D1190974

RETREAT FROM SANITY

RETREAT FROM SANITY
The Structure of Emerging Psychosis

MALCOLM B. BOWERS, JR., M.D.
Associate Professor of Psychiatry
Yale University School of Medicine
New Haven, Connecticut

Human Sciences Press • New York

A Division of Behavioral Publications, Inc.

Library of Congress Catalog Number 73-20296

ISBN: 0-87705-134-8

Copyright © 1974 by Human Sciences Press

Human Sciences Press is a division of
BEHAVIORAL PUBLICATIONS, 72 Fifth Avenue,
New York, New York 10011

Printed in the United States of America
456789 987654321

Library of Congress Cataloging in Publication Data

Bowers, Malcolm B
    Retreat from sanity; the structure of emerging psychosis.

        Bibliography: p. 229
        1. Psychoses. I. Title. [DNLM: 1. Psychoses.
WM200 B786r 1974]
RC512.B67   616.8'9   73-20296

For Natasha, my parents, and
my children

Contents

Preface

This book relies heavily upon the subjective experience of individuals, and I acknowledge foremost the graciousness of my patients in allowing me to share their experiences and, with appropriate safeguards, to publish their accounts. If my interpretation of the accounts is incomplete, the experiences themselves stand here available to others who may be interested in the problem of psychosis.

I owe a major debt in this work to Daniel X. Freedman, M.D., who as clinician and researcher has been a major influence in my professional life. We were coauthors on an earlier paper which has been reworked, and comprises the first chapter of this book. Theodore Lidz, M.D., also an esteemed teacher, has given help and encouragement throughout this endeavor, and has generously contributed the Foreword. Stephen Fleck, M.D., in his own unique way, has been a constant clinical model and exemplar of the kind of patient care that I would like to practice and to teach. I feel a special gratitude to Norma Fox, Senior Editor of Behavioral Publications, whose perseverance and advice at crucial junctures have been indispensable. I heartily thank Lee Baldwin for her typing and editorial assistance with the manuscript.

Some of the sections of this book are revisions of articles I have previously published. I thank the following journals for permission to publish sections of the articles listed: *Archives of General Psychiatry*, Volume 15, pages 240-248, 1966; Volume 19, pages 348-355, 1968; *Psychiatry*, Volume 28, pages 346-358, 1965; *The Human Context*, Volume 3, pages 134-145, 1971.

Malcolm B. Bowers, Jr., M.D.
New Haven, Connecticut
August, 1973.

Foreword

Dr. Bowers has made a major contribution to the study of the psychoses by providing a series of verbatim patient accounts of the experience of becoming psychotic, together with a cogent analysis of the material. Increasingly, the nature and meaning of psychotic states is being clarified by careful scrutiny of the transition to psychoses. Clearer understanding of these phenomena are further guiding our therapeutic efforts. In these few prefatory pages, I wish to consider the book's focus upon patients' experiences and the importance of investigating the period of transition into schizophrenic states.

Although Dr. Bowers has devoted much of his professional life to laboratory investigations, including a search for potential neurochemical reasons for the similarities between drug-induced psychedelic states and schizophrenic psychoses, he has remained alert to what his subjects tell him and has appreciated that people's experiences are as valid a topic for scientific study as the chemistry of their brain metabolism. Here, as in most enduring contributions to the understanding of schizophrenic disorders, the insights derive from careful study of patients' life experiences, a method which serves to remind us of how greatly the study and treatment of such patients have been impeded by the bias which holds that a patient's own ideas concerning what has gone wrong with him are merely epiphenomena of some disorder of the brain.

When we examine the patients' accounts of their experiences, we find that each patient had reached a developmental impasse, confronted by a situation crucial to his development: separation from parental protection and guidance; forming an intimate relationship; coping with homosexual impulses; choosing a career, etc. Caught in the crisis situation and unable to guide himself, he becomes intensely anxious and may fear disintegration. His state of consciousness alters and he becomes hyperalert and flooded by perceptions and memories, and seeks to find directives and meanings in everything. As one subject wrote in retrospect, "My ego was more like a sieve than a control mechanism." In his terrified state, he interprets his environment egocentrically, finding personal significance in everything he encounters or remembers, and he is likely to regress to even earlier types of egocentric cognition and believe that what he thinks and feels influences not only other people, but even the inanimate world. While the precise content of the patient's ideas depends upon his individual experiences, it is, as Dr. Bowers recognizes, often highly stereotyped and basically similar to that of other patients facing the same developmental tasks. In his turmoil or panic, the patient seeks relief by finding answers in what he projects onto his environment or by embracing an "insight" that seems to explain everything, or will be reluctant to continue in his state of uncertainty, indecision, and unbearable conflict. As a medical student who became psychotic wrote (p. 187), "I was really groping to understand what was going on. There was a sequence with my delusions; first, panic, then groping, then elation at having found out . . . When reality started coming back, I became depressed. One part of me seemed to say . . . 'This is a delusion and it will pass.' But the other side of me wanted the delusion, preferred to have things this way.''

Through the material he has collected and his analysis of it, Dr. Bowers has clarified what happens as a person becomes acutely psychotic. He does not commit himself as to the reasons why the patient's state of consciousness alters; he believes it may be due to some innate neurochemical vulnerability, or to the patient's prior experiences including inadequacies or distortions of his upbringing in his family; or to a combination of the two. It is possible that only those persons develop such altered states of consciousness who react to emotional crises with an unusually high output of catecholamines, or by manufacturing abnormal brain amines, etc. However, as Sachar and his associates have shown in their studies of the psychoendocrinology of ego disintegration, which recorded a similar sequence of events at the onset of certain schizophrenic psychoses, the corticosteroid and epinephrine excretions of patients during such turmoil are very greatly elevated. It may be assumed that as part of the response to danger and the massive catecholamine output, the filtering functions of the reticular activating system are lowered. In addition, as I have discussed elsewhere, with the egocentric cognitive regression that takes place, the filtering function of categorical thinking is greatly diminished. It is not clear to me that other reasons for the greatly heightened sensitivity to inner and outer stimuli need be postulated.

We are also confronted by the question of why some persons who experience such breakdowns of defenses find a delusional solution, and abandon reality testing. I have a distinct impression that some individuals in such dilemmas do not, or cannot, become psychotic but rather develop psychosomatic disorders in response to the psychophysiologic imbalance. From studies of the family settings, and particularly, of the styles of communicating and ways of thinking of the parents, it seems likely—at least to some of us—that often the person's poor grounding in reality testing and logical communication within his family leave him vulnerable to psychotic resolution of the altered state of consciousness and the dilemma which initiated it.

It seems important to note that the phenomena described in this book are not typical of all psychotic consciousness, but primarily of early phases of psychoses when the onset is reasonably acute. The thought processes of chronic patients may be very different, with a variety of means of defending against the re-arousal of unbearable feelings and insoluble conflicts—defenses and ways of thinking that have been particularly well described by Maria Lorenz. However, the phases of disturbance considered here are of particular moment to our understanding of psychoses and their therapy. As Dr. Bowers indicates, antipsychotic medications are of major importance in treatment because they diminish the hyperalertness, counter the severe anxiety and tension, and permit the patient to think more calmly and reasonably again. They lessen the need for immediate resolution of dilemma that so often can only be achieved delusionally. Hospitalization is usually valuable, if not essential, because it provides a shelter from insurmountable problems and a moratorium during which alternatives can be considered. As Dr. Bowers emphasizes, the patient also needs therapeutic guidance in gaining the maturity needed to make the essential developmental step—or, if necessary, to come to terms with living within the limitations imposed by his developmental inadequacies. The patients' accounts of their tumultuous and anxiety-ridden states will help overcome the idealization of states of psychotic consciousness that have been fostered by unknowing youths, as well as by a few psychiatrists who should know better. However, Dr. Bowers properly emphasizes that a psychotic experience can be a vital, enriching, and maturing experience when, as is occasionally the case, the patient is fortunate—fortunate in having or finding the person or persons who can help him find his way over the "peak" and back down into a less rarefied and subjective atmosphere in which he can base his future on shared rather than idiosyncratic, egocentric concepts, and live with and gain satisfaction from others.

Theodore Lidz, M.D.

Introduction

For several years I have researched the subjective phenomenology of acute psychotic reactions, an interest which was initially kindled by certain questions which grew out of the study of drug-induced subjective experience. Since most of the information from individuals who had taken psychotomimetic drugs was available only in the form of self-reports, I began to look for comparable accounts from individuals experiencing psychotic reactions which were not related to drug use. I found, to my amazement, that very little material of this type actually existed. I also discovered that individuals on the verge of a psychotic reaction often did write down their thoughts and feelings, so I began to collect these accounts whenever I could. In other instances, I interviewed patients about their own perception of the psychotic experience. While some patients seemed particularly able to articulate the experience, others were not. Further, all the documents which I collected did not, in my opinion, clearly illustrate the form and content of the psychotic experience. Therefore, in the accounts that follow no assumption is made that the selection is random or even representative. I do assume that the documents are valid—that they reflect primarily the individual's honest attempt to represent accurately a tumultuous inner experience rather than a playful or insincere "put on" or dramatic show. On the other hand, there can be no question that the form of the presentation these subjects have made may have been determined by a variety of forces, including desires to master the psychotic state, revel (in some cases) in new-found emotion, and communicate to real or fantasied helpers. Therefore, in this book I have attempted to gather together the most illustrative documents I have collected. It should be noted that the term "psychosis" is used in a particular sense throughout the book. On the one hand, it is restrictive in that "borderline" syndromes are not included; all the patients who are represented in the book were manifestly delusional for days or weeks prior to treatment, and usually required antipsychotic drugs to control their altered state and its psychological concomitants. Yet, in another sense, the term psychosis as used herein is broad, in that no attempt has been made to distinguish between schizophrenic, schizo-affective, and manic-depressive states with delusions.

Some of the accounts are "found objects," that is, unsolicited by anyone so far as is known. Each account was written within one month prior to or following hospitalization or treatment contact. Each individual voluntarily agreed to allow his account to be studied. Other records were obtained from interviews. From two to ten interviews were held with an individual patient, usually some four to eight weeks following hospitalization, after treatment with antipsychotic drugs had been underway for several weeks. We have found that a majority of patients can be interviewed at this time and can present a cogent account of the experiential side of the onset and progression of their psychosis. (Some somatic therapies, including ECT, obliterate memory for the events and feelings leading up to hospitalization. Patients so treated are usually unable to recall or describe their experience of the psychotic state.) As the documents appear here, identifying names and places have been changed to prevent personal identification without alteration of the essence of the narrative. In gathering information I have thus relied essentially upon spontaneous and interview material, and have assumed that such material is trustworthy.

Although not extensive, the literature in this field includes some fascinating documents. A bibliography has appeared which cites many of these sources.[1] Among the classic first person accounts are those by Schreber,[2] Perceval,[3] Custance,[4] Nerval,[5] Boisen,[6] and Lang.[7] A notable collection of patients' experiences has been put together by Kaplan,[8] and by Landis and Mettler.[9] Significant contributions by other professionals include those of Federn,[10] Searles,[11] McGhie,[12] and Chapman and Konrad.[13]

From the beginning of this work my purpose has been to use patient accounts as a data source for the further understanding of psychosis. As I collected and studied my own material and that available in the literature, I began to sense that there was structure and order in psychotic experiences—experiences which might at first glance have appeared totally chaotic and unordered. Thus, these accounts are not intended to place on display the captivating and frightening phenomena of human psychosis; rather, they are presented as one might present the data of a laboratory experiment, with a view toward showing consistency, repetitiousness, and minimal deviation in the data. Therefore, the redundancy found in the accounts is noteworthy. It is precisely this recurrence of pattern which first caught my eye and which I try to convey through the use of the accounts. The fact that psychotic experience has structure is important for the understanding of psychosis. Freud's structuring of neurotic mental life led to advances in therapy and to a kind of humanizing of seemingly bizarre forms of experiences. He himself speculated about the structure of psychotic conciousness:

It may be that the delusions into which these hallucinations are so constantly incorporated may themselves be less independent of the upward drive of the unconscious and the return of the repressed than we usually assume. In the mechanism of a delusion we stress as a rule only two factors: the turning away from the real world and its motive forces on the one hand, and the influence exercised by wish fulfillment on the content of the delusion on the other. But may it not be that the dynamic process is rather that the turning away from reality is exploited by the upward drive of the repressed in order to force its content into consciousness, while the resistances stirred up by this process and the trend to wishfulfillment share the responsibility for the distortion and displacement of what is recollected? This is after all the familiar mechanism of dreams, which intuition has equated with madness from time immemorial.

This view of delusions is not, I think, entirely new but it nevertheless emphasizes a point of view which is not usually brought into the foreground. The essence of it is that there is not only *method* [Freud's italics] in madness, as the poet has already perceived, but also a fragment of *historic truth;* and it is plausible to suppose that the compulsive belief attaching to delusions derives its strength precisely from infantile sources of this kind.[14]

This very probing passage suggests that Freud was intrigued by the possibility that psychotic consciousness was understandable as a complex psychic construct which possessed a content structure similar to that of dreams. The present records are therefore intended to present a view of the structure of psychotic experience. As we can best ascertain clinically, what is the experiential anatomy of the psychotic state? Notions of classification, nosology and etiology have intentionally been put aside with the hope that these issues may ultimately be further illuminated by the phenomenological material presented here.

My working hypothesis has been that acute psychotic experiences are complex subjective states which have three main determinants. First, I suggest that these states share certain general or state-determined characteristics. That is, some aspects of psychotic experience are related to and governed by the altered state itself and can be observed, with certain variations, in many acute psychoses or other altered states of consciousness. These factors may be seen to impart a certain *form* to the experience of psychosis. Experiences of heightened awareness, intensification of sensory experience, broadening of the experiential field of personal relevance, alterations in the sense of self, hypermnesis, externalization of conflict with invasion of various perceptual and cognitive modalities—all would be considered "state-determined" aspects of psychotic experience conferring form upon the experience. A second proposed group of determinants of structure in the psychotic experience are those which are idiosyncratic and related to antecedent individual endowment, experience, conflict, and learning. These factors determine the *content* of psychotic experience. The particular memories evoked, the conflicts and wishes expressed, the growth struggles manifest, and the defensive strategies employed comprise the content of the experience, which is individually derived, as Freud suggests in the passage cited. To varying degrees (which these accounts will illustrate) I suggest that such person-determined issues may initiate and contribute specific content to the form-regulating altered state of the psychotic reaction. Thirdly, I suggest that the life events (including growth tasks) which precede the psychosis can often be understood as specific challenges to areas of individual vulnerability or conflict. Thus, life events and maturational challenges may be seen as determining the *timing* of the psychotic episode. These three components of structure—form, content, and timing—comprise the frame of reference in which the patient accounts are herein presented and analyzed.

Briefly stated, then, the hypothesis is that the individual possessing certain vulnerable character attributes moves through varying developmental stages and life experiences until the immediate configuration of forces is uniquely drawn to exploit his vulnerability. The resulting developmental impasse in certain individuals leads to the altered state of psychosis. This altered state is a complex experiential fabric of rather general form but specific content, as suggested above. The main burden of this book is therefore to illustrate this structure through the use of patient accounts. The analogy to the dream, which Freud proposed, may be apparent. In the dream, individually unique unconscious forces which are thematically related to daily events (analogous to the "immediate configuration of forces" above) achieve direct or symbolic and affective expression at the time of a cyclic neurophysiological event. In psychotic states, over a more protracted period of time, the obligatory demands of development and the vicissitudes of external circumstance may resonate thematically with personality liabilities and conflicts and evoke, in certain individuals, clear or disguised representation of these unconscious issues via a new cognitive pattern—the psychotic altered state of consciousness. The accounts are therefore presented to illustrate the extraordinary and varied blending of state-related, person-related, and event-related mental ingredients.

I feel that the structure of psychotic experience that these accounts support has important implications for theory and treatment of psychotic disorders. In the first place, the notion that an altered state of consciousness prevails in psychotic states is significant. Despite the individual variations which may be encountered, psychotic consciousness is essentially a prolonged and dramatic shift in the way the world and the self are experienced. Modern psychobiologists recognize areas in the central nervous system which subserve such perceptive and apperceptive functions. Further, psychopharmacologists acknowledge the fact that comparable transient and prolonged altered states of consciousness can be produced by a uniquely narrow range of chemical compounds. Thus a psychobiology of some altered states closely resembling some states of psychotic consciousness appears at hand. Such knowledge may indeed lead to a definition of the "end organ deficit" in some individuals prone to psychotic states.

Such knowledge would allow for a new concept of the place of biology or "organicity" in psychotic disorders. Classically, some psychoses have been considered "psychogenic" and others "organic." In the European tradition, the former group usually denoted patients who recovered or fell ill after a definable stress, the latter group those who did not recover and in whose history no stress was identifiable. The notion of liability to an altered state of consciousness, a liability quite likely triggered by psychic conflict, gives birth to new conceptual models in psychotic illness and suggests new psychosomatic relationships in these disorders.

Secondly, the fact that psychic conflict and growth strivings are clearly depicted in psychotic consciousness needs particularly careful analysis. Recently, the novel and provocative "input" experienced in drug-induced states and non-drug-induced psychotic states has led to new approaches to treatment. Using large doses of "psychedelic" drugs, investigators have sought to bring patients to a single life-changing experience. Using smaller doses of these compounds, others have attempted to facilitate the emergence of conflict-laden material in more conventional psychotherapeutic settings. In the area of treatment of psychotic states, R. D. Laing has been a major proponent of the notion that psychotic consciousness should be supported and guided as an avenue to recovery and should not be attenuated by antipsychotic drugs. This approach has gained some acceptance, particularly in the United States. The central controversial issue in these approaches, it seems to me, is the matter of the readiness and the capacity of the individual personality for the assimilation of new cognitive and affective material. As these accounts suggest, the appearance of dynamically important material in consciousness is no guarantee that such material can be rapidly made to work in the life of the patient. My own experience with psychotic patients and that of many colleagues suggests that growth in such individuals is slow and rarely usefully achieved at "psychedelic" moments which may occur in the course of emerging psychosis. Such moments may function as instances of revelation of ultimate capacity. Too often, however, they serve as seductive excuses to avoid the protracted work and pain involved in psychological growth. Further, in our experience, manpower and nurturing are needed, not only during the acute episodes, but perhaps more importantly over the protracted period of years, during which time the individual, no longer actively psychotic, will attempt to build self-confidence, achieve social relationships, and find himself as a competent, acceptable human being. Programs to support such activities are usually poorly supported.

I make no claims that the kind of clinical procedure employed in these accounts is without pitfalls. What is lost on the side of objectivity is gained on the side of involvement. One strong bias running throughout this work, therefore, is one which holds that to understand acute psychotic reactions one should optimally have some contact over time with individuals in whom these reactions occur. Another is that patients who suffer psychotic reactions are very much like other people who have problems in living. My experience had led me to avoid the extremes of the attitudes toward psychosis which have always been prevalent. On the one hand (despite noteworthy and vitally important properties of specialness), people with psychotic reaction patterns are motivated in much the same fashion as other human beings. On the other hand (despite their frequently observed, unique sensitivity to themselves and others) such individuals, in my experience, neither warrant nor benefit from attitudes which celebrate or extol these traits. The attitudes of the extremes have always led to poor care for individuals with psychotic reaction patterns. They have thereby been seen as either vastly alien and incurable (Kraepelin) or strangely gifted and inviolate (Laing). Both attitudes ultimately justify policies of neglect for the majority of patients by mental health personnel and by society.

1. The Altered State in Acute Psychosis

The patient accounts to be related in subsequent chapters will attempt to illustrate our hypothesis that acute psychotic experience is a complex construct containing elements of the past and present which are uniquely felt and portrayed through the permissive mechanism of an altered state of consciousness. This mechanism is evoked initially in some individuals at periods of developmental impasse. By the term "altered state" we mean a prolonged period during which the experience of self and external world are radically altered, when the form and content of conscious experience undergo a profound destructuring. Some aspects of these states will be illustrated in the detailed patients' accounts to follow. At this juncture we will focus on particular generic forms which we have encountered. Although the last word on the phenomenology of psychotic states has not been heard, we feel that, descriptively speaking, two major kinds of experiences can be observed. We do not know whether these kinds of experiences have prognostic significance although some research suggests that they may.[1] Both kinds can be observed in the same patient. These states, despite qualitative differences, are modes of self-experience in which the capacity of the self to control, recognize, and properly "own" or organize the experiential world is markedly diminished. The first type of experience we have termed "psychedelic" to denote the overload character of such states.

"PSYCHEDELIC" EXPERIENCES IN ACUTE PSYCHOTIC STATES

Case 1—A 38-year-old music teacher, pressed by debts and family problems and concerned with a very real national crisis, began to feel that life was taking on a new emotional intensity. He noted a cross on a familiar church for the first time, and felt that it had profound, exciting meaning for him. He felt close to nature, empathically understanding human and subhuman life. A few nights later he described a sensation that "God actually touched my heart. The next day was horror and ecstasy. I began to feel that I might be the agent of some spiritual reawakening. The emotional intensity of the experience became overpowering." Gradually, anxiety and persecutory delusions outstripped the ecstatic elements and the patient made a serious suicide attempt. Even much later in psychotherapy he recalled "the experience" as one of profound meaning for him, one which he would always cherish.

Case 2—A 21-year old college student, concerned about his parents and about a love affair, became guilt-ridden after a sexual experience with his girlfriend. Soon thereafter, he felt that his life was completely changed. He felt a sense of mission in the world which he now saw "as a completely wonderful place" and stated, "I began to experience goodness and love for the first time." Life for him took on an intense benevolent quality which he had never felt before. He talked with friends fervently about the "new life," and about the way he could now care for and understand people. The feelings progressed to frank delusions that he was a religious messiah and heralded an acute catatonic psychosis.

Case 3—Another 21-year-old college student had been ruminating for some time about "personality problems" and difficulties in choosing a vocation. The following is essentially a verbatim account of the week prior to his admission.

Before last week, I was quite closed about my emotions; then finally I owned up to them with another person. I began to speak without thinking beforehand and what came out showed an awareness of human beings and God. I could feel deeply about other people. We felt connected. The side which had been suppressing emotions did not seem to be the real one. I was in a higher and higher state of exhilaration and awareness. Things people said had hidden meaning. They said things that applied to life. Everything that was real seemed to make sense. I had a great awareness of life, truth, and God. I went to church and suddenly all parts of the service made sense. My senses were sharpened. I became fascinated by the little insignificant things around me. There was an additional awareness of the world that would do artists, architects, and painters good. I ended up being too emotional, but I felt very much at home with myself, very much at ease. It gave me a great feeling of power. It was not a case of seeing more broadly but deeper. I was losing touch with the outside world and lost my sense of time. There was a fog around me in some sense, and

I felt half asleep. I could see more deeply into problems than other people had and would go directly into a deeper subject with a person. I had the feeling I loved everybody in the world. Sharing emotions was like wiping the shadow away, wiping a false face. I thought I might wake up from a nightmare; ideas were pulsating through me. I became concerned that I might get violent so I called the doctor.

On admission this patient was severely agitated; delusional and self-referential thoughts were prominent.

Case 4—A 21-year-old student, progressively agitated by homosexual concerns and fears of nuclear disaster, walked all night long with a friend. He described his experience as a "revelation." Sights and sounds possessed a keenness that he had never experienced before. He felt an unusual sense of empathy with this friend and spoke of spontaneous understanding "like that of a little child." Stars in the sky seemed to have special significance, and at one point he felt that his friend resembled Christ. This state proceeded rapidly to an acute catatonic reaction.

Case 5—A 35-year-old housewife sought psychiatric assistance because of her uneasiness over an impending move to another city. In the course of the evaluation she began to wonder about the "meaning of my whole life." She reported sensations of "being a spectator while the procession of life goes by." Over a two-day period her anxiety mounted as she attempted to deal with her guilt about a longstanding affair of which her husband had no knowledge. Rather abruptly she noted "my senses were sharpened, sounds were more intense and I could see with greater clarity; everything seemed very clear to me. Even my sense of taste seemed more acute. Things began to fall together and make sense. Words I would repeat had particular significance for my life." She began to feel that God was asking her to give her life to tell other people about religion. These subjective changes were associated with intense fright and acute insomnia.

Case 6—A 20-year-old artist, who was subsequently followed for seven years in psychotherapy, has frequently referred to his states of altered awareness. Such subjective feelings occurred during each of two acute psychotic episodes and throughout psychotherapy. He describes a mystic or "cryptic state" during which the solutions to various problems seem obvious. Colors become impressive to him, they lose their boundaries, and seem to flow. In these states his sense of communion and community is enhanced; he feels capable of bringing together the arts and sciences, his separated parents, and himself into harmonious "oscillation" with the world. Going without sleep heightens the mystic states and improves his "freedom and vision" in painting. In this state he cannot tell whether he is "thrilled, frightened, pained, or anxious—they are all the same."

Our experience suggests that the fullblown syndrome of amphetamine psychosis often develops out of a state of hyperawareness. One patient, having taken small doses of amphetamine for only three days in the postpartum period, began to have the subjective feeling that God was trying to help her. Colors and normally trivial observations began to take on ominous significance. Things that would not usually be noticed seemed to be "connected." Another patient, chronically sleepless and taking high doses of amphetamines over several months phoned and reported he was feeling better, "released," and productive; the world looked beautiful and bright, he could see "how to repair my marriage" and had new ideas for his work. The next day he reported at length that it was fascinating to note "reflections" from polished cars, and the following day announced that huge parabolic mirrors had been placed on top of a newspaper building and, as a hoax, were reflecting images of naked women off windows and onto bodies. He thus moved from an absorption in the reflections and in his subjective state of "seeing solutions," to problems, to a full-fledged paranoid psychosis.

Case 7—The final case, a young man who had taken lysergic acid diethylamide (LSD-25) two years prior to his psychotic episode, presented a unique opportunity to compare a drug reaction with a psychotic reaction. During his four months of treatment with one of us, he himself frequently compared the two experiences, and found a number of similarities. In his account which follows, the first part was written down after a few weeks of treatment when he was considerably calmer, and was reflecting upon the prior LSD-25 experience. The last part is taken from his admission interview.

In the half hour for the drug to take effect, the drugged person has a psychosomatic terror of madness. He seeks to retain some small part of his former existence unchanged . . . he desires to repeat things for the assurance such repetition gives of a return to normality. The tendency to repeat is compulsive and persistent. There is yet another resistance and that is verbosity. The drugged person, like the insane, feels that weeding out what was previously wrong—an attempt to perfect an earlier feeling—is necessary. There is a paranoid fear of certain places . . . the feeling is that such places are in some way taboo. There are manic feelings under the drug. There are moments when the feeling of omniscience if not omnipotence becomes dominant. The feeling of omnipotence under LSD-25 corresponds directly in intensity to the drugged person's sense of guilt as the drug wears off. The guilt felt afterward can be terribly profound to the point that the depressed person (drugged and/or insane) will do almost anything to bring himself out of the depression. The drugged person, like the insane, is quite vulnerable to suggestion. The experience also involves feelings such as the conviction that one can go through walls. Colors seem to hold great and uncanny significance. All of them are providential and mean something . . . now [on the day he was hospitalized for psychosis] everything takes on significance and patterns. You feel lost and you try to repeat. I feel surges of warmth and great terror of myself. Walls start to move at the periphery of my vision. I feel my tactile senses are enhanced as well as my visual ones, to a point of great power. Patterns and designs begin to distinguish themselves and take on significance. This is true for the LSD-25 experience also. It's the same now as it was with the drug, only then I knew I was coming back. Now there is nothing to hold onto.

Literary Accounts of "Psychedelic" Experiences in Psychotic States

John Custance[2]—First and foremost comes a general sense of intense well-being . . . the pleasurable and sometimes ecstatic feeling tone remains as a sort of permanent background . . . closely allied with this permanent background is . . . the "heightened sense of reality." If I am to judge by my own experience, this "heightened sense of reality" consists of a considerable number of related sensations, the net result of which is that the outer world makes a much more vivid and intense impression on me than usual . . . The first thing I note is the peculiar appearances of the lights . . . They are not exactly brighter, but deeper, more intense, perhaps a trifle more ruddy than usual. Certainly my sense of touch is heightened . . . My hearing appears to be more sensitive, and I am able to take in without disturbance or distraction many different sound impressions at the same time . . . It is actually a sense of communion, in the first place with God, and in the second place with all mankind, indeed with all creation . . . The sense of communication extends to all fellow creatures with whom I come in contact; it is not merely ideal or imaginative but has a practical effect on my conduct.

Anonymous[3]—I experienced a sudden feeling of creative release before my illness, was convinced that I was rapidly attaining the height of my intellectual powers, and that for the first time in my life, I would be able to function up to the level of my ability in this direction . . . On several occasions my eyes became markedly oversensitive to light. Ordinary colors appeared to be much too bright, and sunlight seemed dazzling in intensity . . . I also had a sense of discovery, creative excitement, and intense, at times mystical inspiration in intervals where there was relief from fear . . . My capacities for aesthetic appreciation and heightened sensory receptiveness, for vivid grasp of the qualities of living, and for imaginative empathy were very keen at this time. I had had the same intensity of experience at other times when I was perfectly normal, but such periods were not sustained for as long, and had also been integrated with feelings of well-being and happiness that were absent during the tense, disturbed period.

Schreber[4]—[Dr. Weber, who was in charge of the asylum where Schreber was hospitalized wrote the following in his court testimony:]

At the beginning of his stay there he [Schreber] mentioned mostly hypochondriacal ideas . . . but ideas of persecution soon appeared in the disease picture, based on hallucinations, which at first appeared sporadically while simultaneously marked hyperesthesia, great sensitivity to light and noise made their appearance. Later the visual and auditory hallucinations multiplied and, in conjunction with disturbances of common sensation, ruled his whole feeling and thinking . . . Gradually, the delusions took on a mystical and religious character . . . he saw "miracles," heard "holy music" . . . I have in no way assumed *a priori* the pathological nature of these ideas, but rather tried to show from the history of the patient's illness how the appellant first suffered from severe hyperesthesia, hypersensitivity to light and noise . . . and particular disturbances of common sensation which falsified his conception of things . . . and how from these pathological events, at last the system of ideas was formed which the appellant has recounted . . . in his memoirs.

Clifford Beers[5]—[Beers described the unusual sensory experiences that occurred at the onset of his psychosis:]

While I was at Grace Hospital it was my sense of hearing which was the most disturbed. Soon after I was placed in my room at home all of my senses became perverted . . . The tricks played upon me by my perverted senses of taste, touch, smell, and sight were the source of great mental anguish. None of my food had its usual flavor. This soon led to that common delusion that some of it contained poison . . . At breakfast I had cantaloupe, liberally sprinkled with salt. The salt seemed to pucker my mouth, and I believed it to be powdered alum. Usually, with my supper, sliced peaches were served. Though there was sugar on the peaches, salt would have done as well. Salt, sugar, and powdered alum had become the same to me.

Familiar materials had acquired a different "feel." In the dark, the bed sheets at times seemed like silk . . . What that purpose was I could not divine, and my very inability to arrive at a satisfactory conclusion stimulated my brain to the assembling of disturbing thoughts in an almost endless train. Thus does a perverted sense grow by what it feeds on . . .

My sense of sight was subjected to many weird and uncanny effects. Phantasmagoric visions made their visitations throughout the night . . . Moving pictures, often brilliantly colored, were thrown on the ceiling of my room and sometimes on the sheets of my bed . . . I remember one vision of vivid beauty. Swarms of butterflies and large and gorgeous moths appeared on the sheets. That sight I really enjoyed, knowing that the pretty creatures were not alive; and I wished that the usually unkind operator would continue to minister to my aesthetic taste by feeding it on colors so rich and so faultlessly combined.

Norma McDonald[6]—What I do want to explain, if I can, is the exaggerated state of awareness in which I lived before, during, and after my acute illness. At first it was as if parts of my brain "awoke" which had been dormant, and I became interested in a wide assortment of people, events, places, and ideas which normally would make no impression on me. Not knowing that I was ill, I made no attempt to understand what was happening, but felt that there was some overwhelming significance in all this, produced either by God or Satan, and I felt that I was duty-bound to ponder on each of these new interests, and the more I pondered, the worse it became. The walk of a stranger on the street could be a "sign" to me which I must interpret. Every face in the windows of a passing streetcar would be engraved on my mind, all of them concentrating on me and trying to pass me some sort of message. Now, many years later, I can appreciate what had happened. Each of us is capable of coping with a large number of stimuli invading or being through any one of the senses . . . it is obvious that we would be incapable of carrying on any of our daily activities if even one hundredth of all these available stimuli invaded us at once. So the mind must have a filter which functions without our conscious thought, sorting stimuli and allowing only those which are relevant to the situation in hand to disturb consciousness. And this filter must be working at maximum efficiency at all times, particularly when we require a high degree of concentration. What had happened to me in Toronto was a breakdown in the filter . . . new significance in people and places was not particularly unpleasant, though it got badly in the way of my work, but the significance of the real or imagined feelings of people was very painful . . . In this state, delusions can very easily take root and begin to grow . . . By the time I was admitted to the hospital I had reached a stage of "wakefulness" when the brilliance of light on a window sill or the color of blue in the sky would be so important it could make me cry. I had very little ability to sort the relevant from the irrelevant. The filter had broken down. Completely unrelated events became intricately connected in my mind.

In brief, it seems that these patients are describing a state, which occurred early in their illness, in which they recognize an altered way of experiencing themselves, others, and the world. They report having stepped beyond the restrictions of their usual state of awareness. Perceptual modes seem heightened and changed; the emotional response evoked is singularly intense. Such experiences are frequently felt to be a kind of breakthrough, characterized by words and phrases such as "release" or "new creativity." Individuals experience feelings of getting to the essence of things—of the external world, of others, and of themselves. On the other hand, there is usually a vague, disquieting, progressive sense of dread, which may eventually dominate the entire experience. In some accounts, the experience of perceptual alteration seems to be dominant; others emphasize the intense affectivity, and still others the inner experience of revelation or creative clarification. The term "psychedelic" (mind manifesting) has been applied to some aspects of these experiences with some justification. For whatever the ultimate meaning and assimilation of such manifest subjective data, the experience is intrinsically one of increased sensory pace and content. As we have seen, the notion that some dormant aspects of mental life are being awakened is overdetermined in these experiences. External stimuli impinge more intensely, and the internal tracking of thoughts and percepts increases. Feelings long forgotten may return, and particular life events may be re-experienced with clarity. The externalization of conflict sets up an experiential state in which meaning is purchased at any price. The sense of self may undergo novel and bizarre distortion in consciousness, and affective "pitch" is frequently heightened. All of these ingredients contribute to the ultimate sense that something new and portentous is at hand.

It is important to consider the primary changes in perceptual experiences as distinct from their inclusion in one or another delusional idea. The statement by Dr. Weber, Schreber's physician, is a particularly astute observation of the sequential steps in the formation of delusions. Weber insists that Schreber first experienced "disturbances of common sensation," and the quotation from Clifford Beers is an illustrative example of the same phenomenon. With regard to the special senses, we have been able to observe at least three modes of sensory disturbance. These may be illustrated in part, by the sensory experiences recounted by the following patient. She is a 35-year-old woman with a recurrent psychotic disorder, who has been followed by me for several years. At the beginning of one recent partial relapse she noted the following olfactory phenomena:

> During the time I was getting sick again, I began to think about the abortions I had before I was married. I was feeling guilty about them again. In those days you always tried to abort yourself first by taking quinine. When I was taking a shower and thinking about the past, I suddenly noticed the unmistakable smell of quinine. Soon after that, my mother and I were

> talking and she said something about oranges.
> I immediately began to smell oranges myself.

Thus, in addition to hyperesthesia, there are other kinds of distortion of special sensory experiences in early psychosis. Sensation may be uniquely tied to dynamically significant material, as in the account cited above. Sensory changes in one modality may also be triggered by input from another modality. In the case above, hearing the word *oranges* led to the olfactory experience of oranges.

FRAGMENTED SELF-EXPERIENCES IN ACUTE PSYCHOTIC STATES

In the second type of experience we have seen in psychosis, the experiential self and its sense of ownership and agency may be altered, invaded, divided, or diminished. Whereas the psychedelic experience confronts the experiential self with increased sensory pace and content, in the fragmented self-experience there is a loss of cohesiveness and unity, both in the actual sense of self (identity feeling) and in those cognitive experiences normally "felt" to be one's own and under one's own control.

Case 1—A 20-year-old man was admitted because of profound withdrawal and blocking speech behavior which had been progressive for at least a year. During interviews he would begin to answer questions, but would hesitate painfully, often in the middle of a sentence. Months later he described this inability to finish sentences as due to lapses in his thinking, periods during social interaction when his mind would go blank, as if his thoughts had been "stolen or removed."

Case 2—A 19-year-old man developed acute psychotic symptoms characterized by the notion that he could read the minds of others, or, more precisely, that the thoughts of others simply became his thoughts. He would state that when he noted a particular feeling or expression in someone else, he suddenly realized that "this was my thought too."

Case 3—An 18-year-old girl was admitted in an acute psychotic condition. She was extremely uncommunicative but was suffering visibly from inner turmoil. When she was finally able to describe her state of mind, she said that she felt a part of her had died, that she had "lost the feeling of myself, I am no longer me."

Case 4—A 21-year-old woman developed an acute psychotic reaction in which she felt she was "visited" in her mind by a group of three individuals who told her what to think. When these individuals would decide what thought she should have, then she would experience that very thought.

Case 5—A 20-year-old man developed a prolonged psychotic reaction following an LSD experience. During the acute drug experience, he felt that other people in the room could monitor his thoughts and would react knowingly to them by making certain confirmatory gestures. This state of mind persisted for several months.

Case 6—A 20-year-old woman became acutely psychotic a few weeks after leaving home for the first time to attend college. She, at first, had the notion that a few other people were talking about her. Later she developed the notion that essentially she no longer had any intrapsychic privacy. That is, she felt that her every thought or idea was immediately known to everyone in her immediate social environment. This notion progressed to the idea that her thoughts were literally "broadcast" for all the world to hear. Thought "broadcasting" has been thought to be a symptom of "true" schizophrenia. For this patient the experience was profoundly painful since it was accompanied by intense feelings of shame. A serious suicide attempt was made while she was in the midst of this altered self-experience.

Some investigators feel that these phenomena, characterized by loss of a sense of ownership of thoughts and bodily feeling and by severe alteration in identity feeling, are characteristic of true schizophrenia, in contrast to the schizophreniform states which seem to have a better prognosis. Even at the descriptive level, these experiences represent a more basic alteration in core personality or ego function than the psychedelic type described previously. However, whether this difference has its foundation in the ego organization of the individual or in the psychobiology of the altered state is unknown.

CONTINUITY BETWEEN ACUTE PSYCHOTIC STATES AND OTHER ALTERED STATES

When seen from the point of view of subjective experience some experiencing in the early stages of psychosis becomes less discontinuous with other altered modes of experiencing. For instance, LSD-25 and mescaline may induce a very comparable perceptual and affective condition. The drug state is clearly a multipotential state with many factors influencing the final outcome; an outcome which can range from excruciating anxiety and paranoid delusions to an experience of intense self-knowledge. Space does not permit detailed excerpts from the drug literature, but Terrill's summary of "The Nature of the LSD Experience" can serve as a comprehensive statement of the phenomenon.[7] Such characteristics as increased perceptual sensitivity and portentousness, intensification of interpersonal experience, feelings of unique insight into life, and personal clarification—all well-documented in the LSD reaction—are clearly shared by the accounts we have listed. More recent reviews have made it clear that the drugs induce a kind of fluid state in which a number of variables act to fashion the final result along the psychedelic-psychotomimetic continuum. Giarman & Freedman have characterized this state from the viewpoint of the clinician.[8]

> Psychotomimetic drugs such as d-lysergic acid diethylamide . . . reliably and consistently produce periods of altered perception and experience without clouded consciousness or marked physiological changes; mental processes that are usually dormant and transient during wakefulness become "locked" into a persistent state. The usual boundaries which structure thought and perception become fluid; awareness becomes vivid while control over input is markedly diminished; customary inputs and modes of thought and perception become novel, illusory, and portentous; and with the loss of customary controlling anchors, dependence on the surroundings, on prior expectations, or on a mystique for structure and support is enhanced. Psychiatrists recognize these primary changes as a background state out of which a number of secondary psychological

states can ensue, depending on motive, capacity, and circumstance. This is reflected in the terminology that has grown around these drugs; if symptoms ensue, the term psychotomimetic or psychodysleptic is used; and if mystical experience, religious conversion, or a therapeutic change in behavior is stressed, the term psychedelic or mind "manifesting" has been applied.

There are other intense self-experiences which have elements in common with the accounts we have presented. William James's classic study of religious phenomena, for instance, is replete with accounts of conversion experiences that are strikingly similar to the cases we have described, and to the experiences of some subjects under LSD-25 and mescaline.[9] James describes the characteristics of the affective experience in religious conversion as follows:

> The central one is the loss of all worry, the sense that all is ultimately well with one, the peace, the harmony, the willingness to be, even though the outer conditions should remain the same . . . The second feature is the sense of perceiving truths not known before. The mysteries of life become lucid . . . and often the solution is more or less unutterable in words . . . A third peculiarity of the assurance state is the objective change which the world often appears to undergo . . . The most characteristic of all the elements of the conversion crisis . . . is the ecstasy of happiness produced.

James himself seems to have been well aware of the similarity between the conversion experience and certain psychotic reactions.

But more remains to be told, for religious mysticism is only one half of mysticism. The other half has no accumulated traditions, except those which the textbooks on insanity supply. Open any one of these, and you will find abundant cases in which "mystical ideas" are cited as characteristic symptoms of enfeebled or deluded states of mind. In delusional insanity . . . we may have a diabolical mysticism, a sort of religious mysticism turned upside down. The same sense of ineffable importance in the smallest events, the same texts and words coming with new meanings, the same voices and visions and leadings and missions, the same controlling by extraneous powers; only this time the emotion is pessimistic: instead of consolations we have desolations; the meanings are dreadful; and the powers are enemies to life. It is evident that from the point of view of their psychological mechanism, the classic mysticism and these lower mysticisms spring from the same mental level, from the great subliminal or transmarginal region of which science is beginning to admit the existence, but of which so little is really known. That region contains every kind of matter: "seraph and snake" abide there side by side. To come from thence is no infallible credential. What comes must be sifted and tested, and run the gauntlet of confrontation with the total context of experience, just like what comes from the outer world of sense.

The significance of religious feeling in psychosis has been earlier explored by Boisen[10] and more recently by Laing.[11] Maslow has described the subjective phenomenology of "peak experiences," and emphasizes new modes of awareness which may be encountered at certain maturational milestones.[12] Similarly, in the course of psychotherapy, crisis points and periods of intense insight may also be characterized by exhilaration, expressed new modes of experiencing and perceiving, transient fear mixed with intense happiness, and a sense of acceleration of intrapsychic activity. [13/14] Mystical experiences occurring as a culmination of intense intrapsychic conflict have recently been presented.[15] The utility of such insight, the extent to which it is delusional or adaptive, varies not only in psychotherapy but in psychoses, drug states, and religious and mystical states.

With the advent of psychotomimetic drugs there was renewed interest in the study of altered mental states, but the opportunity to catch *in situ* the formation and genesis of a variety of symptoms and modes of behaving and coping has not been extensively exploited. In part, it was doubted that drug-induced experiences were sufficiently related to clinically encountered dysfunctions to be of interest.[16] Yet, it is hardly surprising that temporary and experimentally induced states do not reproduce all the features characterizing clinical processes; the latter are neither bound as rigorously by time nor circumscribed by the highly socialized safeguards of the conventional laboratory situation. Rather, these differences only highlight those features of clinical disorders which require explanation in terms of developmental factors and restitutive and compensatory sequences. The patient experiencing and functioning in this altered state must cope over time with a variety of life tasks, family and social interactions; his resilience and overall disposition to represent, identify, and differentiate "inside and outside" and to relate in a reality-oriented way, will distinguish him from most experimental subjects.

Similarly, the fact that these drugs produce ecstatic states from which new learning, a shift in values, or subsequent behavior change purportedly ensue, was thought to isolate such states from their "psychotomimetic status," and perhaps to elevate them to a higher level of discourse. Some enthusiasts even appear to argue that this novelty is beyond psychological description and investigation. Yet the variety of contexts in which such mystic states occur includes psychotic illnesses, as our data have reemphasized. It is also evident that this range of similar states differs not only in outcome, but in the extent to which a variety of ego functions are operative—functions such as memory, self-reflective capacity, tolerance for ambiguity, selective attention, the ability to implement wishes and needs in reality, the ability to synthesize, to order, and to serially locate, and to integrate ongoing experiences with past and future. These differentiating features tend to be lost if all such states are described only in terms of loosened ego boundaries, regression in the service of the ego, altered ego autonomy, and deautomatization. [17/18] Such descriptions should properly apply only to certain aspects and attributes of certain of the ego operations altered during these conditions. During various phases of the clinical course of a psychosis, one frequently sees fluid states in which elements of perceptual instability and psychedelic experience occur, preceded or followed by more settled postures in which the patient, through either recognition, insight, withdrawal, or delusion and symptom formation, tends to experience and cope in quite different ways. Similarly, in drug-induced psychedelic states, as the acute and vivid effects subside, one can observe a variety of paranoid and defensive measures, mild ideas of reference, mood change, and inappropriate or highly imaginative interpretations of the ongoing or previous experience. From a descriptive and theoretical standpoint, then, the clinical and drug-induced psychedelic experience reflects a multipotential mental state which cannot easily be encapsulated or understood without careful scrutiny and study of the sequences of states and differentiation of primary and secondary reactions. It seems apparent that the reaction of the therapist or other significant persons in the environment could crucially affect the course and resolution of such states.

Descriptively, these states of heightened awareness but diminished control over input are frequently characterized by delusional mastery (either shared or idiosyncratic) or (as with dreams) by hallucinatory mastery of the ongoing experience with concomitant euphoria. One is reminded of Freud's "model psychosis." "A dream, then, is a psychosis," he remarked, beginning a chapter in the *Outline of Psychoanalysis*.[19] The absurdities, lapses, hallucinatory mastery, and mental processes of psychoses are evident in dreams, Freud argued. Some of the differences between dream and psychosis cited by him were the short duration of the dream, its useful or adaptive function, and the fact that it is to some degree under the control of the dreamer. In the case of drug-induced states, the onset and duration of changes (and to a great extent the intensity of effects) are dependent on dosage. On the other hand, as Freud noted, "the dream is brought about with the subject's consent and is ended by an act of his will." However, this might be translated into the language of ego psychology: the dream as an episode in a sequence of states is implied as is a normal, overall capacity to integrate this episode into the total fabric of living. Such autonomy or integrative control probably is present in widely varying degrees in the states we have reviewed.

These states frequently appear almost to compel rationalization or interpretation as, on occasion, do dreams or any number of traumatic, infantile, or hypnoid states[20] in which the ongoing intense experiences have yet to "run the gauntlet of confrontation" with total experience. That this is not easy, and that delusional outcomes, conversion, or startling change in behavioral patterns can occur, is apparent. These outcomes occur with varying degrees of dependence upon persons, groups, or authority. Thus, this kind of experience is highly narcissistic (in that it is referred to the self), but descriptively, certain aspects of relatedness to objects remain, and even attain a heightened personal significance; further, such relatedness assumes a heightened importance in regulating ego functions. In the drug experience, subjects characteristically depend on the therapist or "guide" not simply as an object, but for elemental ego support—to diminish anxiety and to structure the experience or to sanction participation in it. Patients in acute psychotic states have similar needs for ego support. From scrutiny of clinical and drug-induced states one might propose that there is a rearrangement of a number of ego functions (of which changes in the control of sensory data, attention, perception, and stability of mental self-representation are quite striking); these may lead subsequently or concomitantly to a narcissistically enhanced sense of the self or to a markedly distorted sense of the self and the world. The experimental production of experiences of altered awareness can help both to differentiate and reveal the relatedness of many complex phenomena encountered in clinical psychiatry, with their intricate layering of social, motivational, compensatory, and regressive features. The wide range of contexts in which states of altered awareness are found to occur and the variety of initiating causes indicate that this mode of functioning and experiencing reflects an innate capacity (like the dream), in a most general sense, of the human mind.

There are a number of drugs which apparently can initiate or trigger a psychotic altered state of consciousness in a predisposed individual. These compounds include the monoamine oxidase inhibitors, tricyclic antidepressant compounds, lysergic acid diethylamide and related indolealkylamines, amphetamine and related compounds, and possibly 1-dihydroxyphenylalanine. (Several patient accounts illustrating psychotic states related to drug use will be presented.) The essential point to be made here is that, if the altered state is dissected out as an ingredient in psychosis, it becomes a concept which can be related to the biology of altered states of consciousness. Thus, one possible model of the "organ vulnerability" in psychosis becomes apparent.

2. Psychosis Associated with Heterosexual Rejection

DAVID

David G., at the time of his hospitalization, was a 21-year-old senior at a Western university. He was approaching the end of his college career with a great deal of concern about his future. Though he had already been accepted by a prominent law school, David was not certain about his choice of vocation, and had also given some consideration to medicine and writing. David knew that his father, a lawyer, had also encountered difficulty in choosing a vocation and had taken a kind of moratorium after college by going abroad to participate in a foreign civil war. The experience had been disillusioning, however, and Mr. G. had given up his idealism completely, directing his attention to making money. In many ways, Mr. G. considered himself a failure, and though he made a good living for his family, he was unhappy with his accomplishments. He had managed to purchase a very expensive home, though there always seemed to be outstanding debts.

Mrs. G., long intimidated by her husband, sought psychiatric assistance for intractable asthma two years before David's hospitalization. As a result she became more assertive toward her husband in ways that frequently took the form of undercutting his authority in the home and belittling his sexual ability. Mr. G. was usually very passive toward his wife, dealing with her aggression with a kind of sarcastic banter. However, following bouts of drinking he would engage in violent outbursts, and on such occasions David, his 18-year-old sister, and his 13-year-old brother were often witnesses to the abusive arguments of their parents. Mrs. G. held the threat of divorce constantly over the heads of other family members.

David had a special girlfriend, Laura, who had been in psychotherapy for two years. Their relationship was characterized by a great deal of sexual experimentation, with David frequently doubting his own sexual ability. Separations and reconciliations were violent, highly-charged experiences, much in the fashion of the relationship between David's parents. In mid-February Laura had dated a boy in another city and refused to tell David the details. He immediately fantasied that Laura had engaged in intercourse with her date and wrote a very vindictive poem to her, calling her a whore. Having mailed the poem, he felt angry and guilty. A trip to another city, where he visited friends, served only to assure David that they had their own troubles. Following his return, he wrote a short story entitled "Test To Be a Man" in which the storyteller finds that his best friend has stolen his sweetheart. He became even more overwrought when he learned that a lifelong friend, Nathan, sided with Laura in her quarrel with David. This discovery prompted him to write Nathan a "hate letter," accusing him of betraying their friendship. At this point, David essentially confined himself to his room at college, attended a few classes, but spent most of his time—day and night—at the typewriter attempting to get his thoughts on paper.

At one point, he seemed to view this process as a self-analysis. He recorded the progress of events in calendar form as follows:

Sunday, Feb. 22-wrote letter to Laura, severing.

Weekend, Feb. 28-fled to Cleveland, no good.

Monday, March 2-wrote story "Test To Be a Man."

Friday, March 6-found Nathan sympathetic to Laura, story comes true.

Sunday & Monday, March 8 & 9-two hate letters to Nathan.

Monday & Tuesday, March 9 & 10-intense anxiety.

Wednesday, March 11-partial solution (intuitive) in letter to Nathan.

Friday, March 13-ended diary.

Saturday, March 14-began self-analysis.

March 17-case closed.

The following day he found his way to the hospital emergency room where he presented a picture of intense fright, pressure of speech, ideas of influence and reference, and autistic thinking. The diagnosis, based on clinical data and psychological tests, was acute, undifferentiated schizophrenic reaction. Later, when his parents visited his room at school, they found the typed account that is reprinted below. There has been some deletion and condensation where certain sections were repetitive, but otherwise the account has not been altered in any way.* The stream-of-consciousness style has been left as written by the patient, who has given his consent for the publication of this material. Brief explanatory footnotes have been included where they seem indicated.

*All the patients' accounts, in this and subsequent chapters, have been transcribed just as they were written, retaining idiosyncratic spelling and punctuation.

SLIGHT DEPRESSION
OR
WATCHING YOURSELF LIVE
OR
JUST A WEEK LIKE ANY OTHER

Monday, March 9, 1964
    She had said she loved me (bopping off to Prov-
idence in between protests I suppose I could swal-
low that though) but I don't think if it were ever
true, that she still does. (N told me that, told me just
like that and the reason he hadn't called was cause
he was playing pickup sticks with her date he's so
charmingly forthright I puke).
    His logic is so good he can laugh at his own [girl]
having her insides torn out he's so positive and rational and knows just how everything works including one divorce, one abortion that he's undoubtedly reassured her everything's all right such a
good friend midwife to disasters a cool guy that's
what so even if she does still love me (she was so
cold on the phone) anyway so cold her voice on the
phone she wanted to chat I fantasied suicide for
twenty-four hours . . . twenty-four hours you begin
to scare yourself like that wanted to chat bragged
she'd burned 'everything' (I wanted to ask if that
everything included thirty dollar cashmeres doubt
it) chat about her date etc. If he had been alone I
would have killed I promise if I believe anything is
left in myself I promise I would have killed but he
was only there as a friend so that solution would
have been disproportionate honor among friends (I
had asked him not to meddle asked him as a friend
ha ha) being outdated anyhow no one not even me
would have understood not being able to kill him

and less able to kill myself I just got drunk alone in Harlem. If she still loves me if then still I can't see her talk to her until I am worthy if I can ever be of her of anything until at least say (stinking symbolism runs my life) even then if I see her at all it must be to propose to say here I am me at last me I respect myself can respect love marry you can bolt myself onto life and ride ride ride we'll ride together some say it's a good thing I'd like to give it a try when I trust myself and what I am when that time comes I shall say I love you.

I have a right I do have a right to hold that bastard responsible . . . my game wasn't pretty perhaps; I wanted her to relent first, that's all, just relent first that much of the double standard I hold by if that means double standard but she bore the burden she ran off on me I had a right . . . she made no attempt at apology that night none none so we're both prideful but all I wanted was an I'm sorry even to the letter I wrote, horrible letter designed to humble and that's all just asking an emotional sacrifice an ego sacrifice on her part something she had been as little willing to make as I was . . . but she couldn't do it with that snake whispering in her ear someone for her anyone for her to talk to excuse herself to but me.*

Tuesday, March 10, 5 A.M.
Story will be turned down today for the simple reason that it's lousy. I don't realize things like that before I've shown them all over town . . . at least then I'd avoid having my vanity take as bad a beat-

*The foregoing passage deals with his presumed betrayal by Laura and Nathan's willingness to be Laura's confidant in the argument.

ing as my pride . . . and there's old Hawthorne's
bosom serpent for you eating away hissing all night
I lie there and I lie there and think and think and
think all the time trying not to think I think anyway or reminisce rather (delightful pastime) until
pow I feel like the top of my head blows off and I
smash my fist into something and begin all over
again like a one cycle engine. As far as the stories go
it's a good thing I'm going to make money as a lawyer. Quite ingenuously it is hard for me to believe I
write so poorly. Hemingway says it should be two
against the world the religion the New Faith and all
nothing like that just her there exclaiming how she
made it or worried about her mother or trying to
beat me in ping pong and when I got off the boat
last fall I announced I was going to rescue and protect her! I'm getting warts on my neck, I deserve
them. Tonight I composed three different suicide
notes in my head and I think I broke the pinkie on
my left hand when the pow came. What a joy if insanity were still the romantic mysterious brain fever
type thing it was in the 19th century then I could try
going mad instead of writing I'd probably be better
at it.

Hemingway lost a whole suitcase full of his earli-
est stories and was thus forced by the world (con-
veniently that world which kills the bravest, gen-
tlest, blest etc.) to start again. Maybe if I can find a
suitcase will get lost. The one real advantage of suicide is that at least there wouldn't be a reception at
the Master's house afterwards. I want a war like
Hemingway had . . . it isn't fair . . . I never learned
to shoot squirrels either.

What a sad thing! There is nobody any good
around anymore . . . I was going to be the last one

and then mucked it. Will spring never come??? Or
maybe they could make insomnia less painful by
changing the time system: IST . . . insomniac sav-
ings time.

March 10, 5 P.M.

   I'm becoming a monomaniac it's incredible it
just doesn't stop there are moments when I can do
no more than tear up matchbooks futile futile
things and others of greater lucidity when I can see
so clearly what went wrong why we were unable to
commit ourselves each coming to the brink at different moments I came to her that evening at her
house felt my insides dissolve with wanting, expecting to burst free she put me off good put me off and
put me off and then 12 hours later when the thing
lay sticky like bile inside me then only then we went
to bed together and she had her orgasm and I did
crossword puzzles. Did she ever come at me yes I
suppose, at the beginning, too fast too desperately
when she knew there was no chance and was doing
it on her doctor's advice and I kept telling her I was
no therapist that wasn't my job not my job. But that
letter should have been a test it was a test I wanted
her to make it on her own without help confronting
everything but she dragged in a surrogate she
dragged in my lily-livered friend and he came gal-
loping to the rescue in all the accoutrements of
maiden rescue and good will. There are moments of
lucidity when I see how close hate and love can lie,
back to back, moment to moment I could kill I
could love I lie here tearing up matchbooks. My
story was rejected and I think I mucked an English
test this morning. Will do the same for a French test
tomorrow. The big test is still ahead or behind I tear

up matchbooks. First a tragedy then a comedy I
keep trying to laugh. Someone said you can refuse a
man a loan you can refuse him your sympathy but
you can't refuse him a fight if he wants to fight. I'll
beat him on the streets I'll beat him in front of
Laura or before his parents. He'll fight. Anyhow at
last that second self is returning the one that wants
to turn his life into a work of art it's returning a
little in writing momentary sweet breaths of sanity
in the end perhaps it's the only way I must write
even poorly.*

Tuesday, March 10, 10 P.M.

I can't cope, I can't come to grips . . . it's Hawthorne's disease blazing away, red guilt or little
stringy black warts (they're growing with a virulence I swear I never noticed before) . . . music helps
a bit and I've conducted the Eroica all over the room
three times already today, waving my arms and occasionally hitting things . . . all very dramatic . . . to
think I worried myself about sleeping too much last
fall! I've given the jargon a once over; it stems from
incest drives, castration fears, masturbation com-
plexes, homosexual doubts, oedipal fixations bullshit bullshit it was around before the jargon and it's
got me . . . already at table I've been making curious
unconscious slips as if the synapses suddenly rot
away and I come disconnected it's all right it's all
right I'm going to be a lawyer and make lots of
money and grow up to be as weak as my father as
torn as my mother look ahead!! Be a good little benjy franklin and don't despair; simply write down

*In these entries he seems preoccupied with his lack of success as a
writer; which was a progressive and painful realization for him.

your virtues on one side of the page like this and then your vices on the other (that's a good boy) now add them up, divide by the fraction of a normal life already lived (that's right, one third) nice going benjy you're doing fine, now multiply by your abilities as scored by the IBM machine and factor by your various ambitions (what's the matter benjy?? haven't got any? Come on now boy, you always did want to invent a lightning rod, didn't you? Or build a fire house? Sure you did . . . well skip it and just multiply by the height of the statue you want built after your death) now . . . what have you got? (now don't be corny benjy, Hemingway has already been through that for you . . . try something else) (be a good boy benjy and don't seek escapes in vulgarity, try again) look here, benjy, we'll have none of your morbidity, be positive boy, reach down way deep inside you and tell the world what you find HATE HATE HATEHATEHATE (what a cornball! A lousy sensationalist . . . what kind of founding father would you make?) Founding father? Are you kidding? I'm well on my way to becoming a blithering schizoid it's too bad really too bad I have too much of a sense of humor to believe that adam eve and apple stuff . . I rather think that Beckett's got the right idea and original sin was trying to climb out of the mud we must have had a good time back then never overreaching, no such thing as hubris or stargazing or breasts the size and texture of (dear diary! How can I begin, you mean I really never tried before? Who was I kidding did I never chance to look in the mirror and see the warts) of Christ the more fool you.

Tuesday, March 10, 11 P.M.

It's silly to stop now, I've got a good rhythm going. I type for twenty minutes and then read back
over the past two months for forty. That makes an
hour. Then I begin again. Pretty soon I'll get sleepy
from all this banging down on the keys and then I'll
go to sleep and start fresh in the morning. I ought
to entitle this to my future headshrinker cause Mr.
White says this is about the age when the snap occurs . . . he says anything can set it off if it's there to
begin with (what that means, of course, he's not
sure . . . I am) any drop in (get this) "esteem in-
come" occasioned by test situations or symbolic maturity crises like graduation, or tests or even a love
affair (what a bland term!) So I'm waiting. Where
and when does it begin? Do you at some point decide to go crouch in a corner talking to yourself unable to shit? Except maybe I'm pulling myself out
of it, kind of reeling out the intestines of it diseased
inch by inch . . . sublimating in otherwords. My
concerns are once again pretentiously self-conscious, I notice in my rereadings an increasing
number of quotes and witticisms . . . I'm showing
off again, what a good thing: Like the eighty-year
old women in the asylum to whom the scientists
gave estrogen just to see what would happen . . .
sure enough, they began combing their hair and fix-
ing their dresses and primping, in short preparing
like mad to go out and have their hymens busted
again. Everybody, doctors and relatives and other
patients thought Oh what a good thing that they're
taking a renewed interest in life! I thought it was a
rather touching thing myself. So I'm taking a renewed interest in life . . . I even began criticizing
certain turns of construction in the pages just written . . . hot diggity, pretty soon I'll be sitting around

in a pile of writing up to my ears and simply tickled pink! Like feces I'll play with the paper make gliders and little sailor hats and be innocent again.*

Rereading this time, I just noticed a terrible thing . . . I'm such a short sighted misanthrope that I will never be able (in a particularly severe paroxysm of self pity of course) to give this to any of my friends . . . There isn't a single one I've spared much less said a good word of! I'm sorry really. The obvious solution is to send it to Laura and then blow my brains in (I'd prefer to fall on a sword but I'd probably take it through the forearm) that way she'd feel bad about burning it. Egotism the bosom serpent, I need a good priest.

Midnight, Tuesday-Wednesday

Every last bit of it, right to the bottom of the stable get out all the crusted horse dung leave it spic and span so there will be place for more. Cause like they say there is knowing and then there is knowing and I know anything at all . . . I know how to type ten hours running and drink beer (thank god the beer was around I'm broke and down to my last two cigars and not a bit sleepy yet) but I don't know what to DO and that's what counts most of all. Or does it? It appears I'm out to prove the cliche about the intellectual . . . except I'm no intellectual so that is solved, or maybe it proves the cliche about the tortured jew, but then I'm no jew either. I sure know all about what I'm not. This little dispatch from hell is really turning in on itself like a seashell

*Here, as in other places, he seems to flirt with the idea of going insane even to the point of addressing, in a sense, his future psychiatrist.

winding smaller and smaller; I see now where I picked up the theme of insanity mentioned flippantly and in passing, and succeeded in running it into the ground . . . I ought to skip the verbiage and go find a good crown of thorns, or do like Bruce did in Cleveland drink somebody's blood and lie back blissfully in their vomit . . . but then he was drunk and that doesn't count and shouldn't discourage the happy people. Boy, that Nathan and Laura business really pulled the cork I'm bad or mad or just dull? Down on my knees before the crescent moon I got my pants dirty. This is undoubtedly one of the most prolix records of a scarring over process (I'm sealing like one of those puncture proof tires, but in slow motion) I should be back to my habitual state of callousness in a couple of days with no apparent damage, maybe I can even go on staving off like this ("a poem is a momentary stay against confusion" Frost . . . this is quite a poem) till I die. I guess you shouldn't be alone in a moment like this, what you need is a good friend . . . ha . . . today he gets the letter, the second letter, the one in which I spoke his own language . . . nothing assauges nothing (oh don't do that again you've already done that twice before, try something new, quote some more big names).

One ray of hope (the first branch, Mt. Arrarat is in sight, get all the animals ready to debark the hell out of here particularly the snakes and spiders) that is my regrets and nostalgias seem to be coming closer on the heels of my debacles last time it took me two years to realize that I'd made a mistake with Laura, this time it took me two weeks, but maybe next time (three strikes you know the pitch?) well maybe next time I will have killed Nathan first . . . a

little foresight should do the trick . . . what drives
that bastard anyway? I think I've taken him to represent my own rational sickness and not seen what
he is at all, it's myself I hate in him . . . but then the
old empirical hard core fact remains that this is the
second time he snivelled around in the wake of my
romance with Laura . . . of course, she begged him
to . . . they can both go to hell (redundancies boy,
esthetic considerations are replacing moral ones for
the sweet sake of sanity and the coming spring) skip
it.

How can I hate myself like this?

Thursday, March 12, 11 A.M.

I'm out! I'm through . . . boomed out of the tunnel sometime last night and it's raining stars . . .
whooey . . . it's nice out there's time for everything
. . . I can do it I did it and if it happens again I'll do
it again twice as hard I got a dexamyl high going
and I'm not on dexamyl and I've been up for forty-
eight or more hours and I'm giddygiddygiddy and I
took a test this morning and it was on Voltaire and I
kicked him a couple of good ones for being down
on Pascal that poor bastard with his shrivelled body
and bottomless abyss they're not bottomless!! You
get down far enough and it gets thick enough and
black enough and then you claw claw claw your
way out and pretty soon you're on top again. And I
licked it by myself, all alone. No pandering psychiatrists or priests or friends by myself. Now, I
must admit I'm a little leery; I dashed back to the
typewriter to give it form to write it down and sew it
in my vest like Pascal so if the Thing hits me again
I'll have this in my vest and I'll kick it in the teeth
again but Pascal saw God and yet still it hit him

again . . . will it hit me again? Who cares . . . I just sat in on one of those weddings of the soul and I tooted tooted . . . I don't care I can use it I can run on it it will be my psychic gasoline now I don't have to sleep sleep all the time to get away with it . . . but if I lose my typewriter? So my hand will get tired too bad. The tail ain't going to wag this dog no more . . . at least not as ferociously. The passions, the humors, the libido, the original sin, the blood curse I'm going to put them all in a suitcase and then I'm going to lose that damn suitcase or maybe I'll just keep throwing it away. But I can do it. I licked this school and I licked my blue bear. Maybe I can even lick Laura . . . she can't do it for herself. Maybe I've got enough left over for two. I took that test without having read three quarters of the material with my head still going whooey and I licked that. Maybe I can lick Laura.*

I got a few confessions to make. Still, I think I did overflow a bit on other people and that is just a trifle bit humiliating since I knew they couldn't help anymore than a psycho and then, yesterday afternoon I trotted over to the third floor of Univ. Health and the woman said Well, we have two openings next week maybe we can fit you in and I thought about that guy who got put off like that and launched himself from the roof and will never fly again and thought for a while how bad I was going to make them feel having history repeat itself and came near to slamming my fist on the receptionist's desk (having made that great sacrifice in the first place . . . ah pride) and nearly shouted That's non-

*This passage exemplifies one of several passages in which some relief and a sense of resolution and clarification break through his mounting anxiety.

sense I just want a little offhand advice this business should be more convenient and stormed out noting on the way a slightly terrified look in the poor receptionist's eye that was fun . . . I can always do that again too if the Blue Bear ever comes growling back. Poor Voltaire, the son of a bitch never understood never did spend a frenetic life throwing well turned witticisms into Pascal's yawning pit and eternal silences ah the sound and the fury I'd better get some sleep now. Or maybe I'm a manic-depressive. Maybe the pills did it to me. It's coming back step on it step on it shave that Blue Bear. No. I've got it now. Just don't reread anything but the good parts. That's it. Underline them.

Oh jesus christ I still don't really believe in anything I just got myself too worn out to care. I'm pretty sure Kierkegaard had something to say about this but if I get any more names and quotes and things in my head my ability to make fun of them is just going to go pachunk and I'll give out altogether. No dice. Me I'm still flying.

The coincidence of my break up with Laura with imminent graduation and the inevitability of law school combined with pressures from home have kicked off these bouts of self-doubt and account for the virulence of the blue bear (subconscious, warts, dreams etc.) White is wrong or Freud or whoever insisted that dreams are pure wish fulfillment . . . or rather, the wish may be very subtle . . . a wish to punish oneself . . . because certainly my greatest wish at the moment is to beat this thing and I certainly haven't dreamed any victories yet. How many years did it take Freud? I'll bet he didn't have any french paper to write for tomorrow. No that's for sure.

But the biggest step has been made . . . I have objectified my disturbances in the person of Blue Bear (we'll deal with that one later) torn them apart from myself in the moment of tooting and prevented them from wrecking me. Now I must destroy the blue bear once and for all.

ANNOUNCEMENT: A new campaign is on against the word "maybe." When I stamp out maybe maybe I'll stop smoking. I tremble seeing how close I came to the brink. How do you like that? I repressed the whole reason for writing this time . . . I knew I had missed something (ha ha won't get away from me blue bear I'm hot on your tail) my story was truer than I wished to believe (changing hair color location and all etc.) I had taken Nathan as symbolic of some male principle and was tormenting myself with . . . he's just as stuck as most of us, he just has great and clever specialized intellectual faculties . . . so that the irony of my story coming semi-true was also too much to take and aggravated my sense of betrayal. That letter to him then was not completely sincere . . . I don't want him to do my courting (that was the doubt about the manliness of the favor) I just wanted to apologize to both of us and maybe duck the decision to go after Laura myself because after all, I'm not sure that I need her if she represents no more than a test. Well, we'll see . . . maybe the test wasn't such a bad idea because if she's got the guts to take me back she's a big enough girl for me and we'll see what comes of it. I was half exposing myself, half proving myself, half boasting to her and hurting her, half admitting my problem and half challenging her to save me . . . no one saves you Christ was a fool you save yourself. Let me qualify that, you don't save yourself all at once up on a cross that's what Nathan would like to do and Pascal and all the absolute hunters craving to die in orgasm before the starry heavens shaking their fists or down on their knees life doesn't work that way . . . novels and poems do and should . . . to live "en bonne foi" in good faith with yourself you have to save yourself each day . . . not in some corny way helping old ladies across the street . . . but in a little soul plunging before breakfast . . . a pickerupper. You can do it with the setting up exercises.

March 12, Midnight

I mustn't test it yet . . . I've got to keep quiet . . . I've got momentum habits of exhibitionism and I've come to grips with my own doubts but the resolution hasn't been strong enough to sustain the doubts of other . . . I can't be a proselytizer because the essence of my discovery is that there ARE NO doctrines that living is a day by day affair I do much better talking about monopoly I LIKE to talk about monopoly I LIKE to touch things and listen to things I CAN'T support Greg's problems I start proving myself to him QUIET QUIET SHUT UP AND SILENCE I can see too well what happens I go on a grand flight and halfway up it sounds hollow and then to save face I begin to force and push and I can carry him along for a minute but he always comes down before I do and then my stomach just caves in . . . the thing is too fragile to test yet . . . if it were only based on a permanent thing on an absolute on God capital g on Love capital L but it isn't and I don't want it to be even Fromm became a doctrinaire and then he was no good anymore I wish I could pray god give me just a couple of years of this that is all that will be enough I am so big now my body has such stretching potential it gallops like Thomas Wolfe's character it bounds along and it doesn't touch ground until someone like Greg casts a shadow.*

I must pursue the analysis and not talk about it. I know what I must do. Right now, with eight hours to go I must stay awake (I feel like I've been up for two weeks) and do the french paper . . . Laura once said it is going to be fun falling in love with you I was flattered but I didn't understand now I do . . . what do they say? Take it as it comes? Right that's it . . . just take it as it comes too bad we didn't . . . too bad? What am I saying . . . a damn tragedy . . .

HUMILITY let's go right back to the text books right back to the puritan primers cause after all they know what they were talking about and if I've done it then what I've done is to secularize and personalize their solution and I must keep my trap shut.

But jesus I feel that I've changed I really do I've never felt this way before I'm even beginning to trust it a little bit . . . so if you are introspective then BE introspective . . . all the way . . . you come through the bottom and out the other side and there's a world out there just waiting to be eaten played on lived with worked for jumped up and down upon made love to sung about man I'm six years old.

I could be simply overawed but in rereading this I see an incredible, an astonishing structure . . . automatic writing but there is development, there is almost an internal plot . . . the hand of god? Or of

*Greg is an acquaintance who occasionally drops in to visit as David types out his thoughts.

the subconscious? Or of both at the same time? Grace and peace and inner peace. Or have I gone mad? Am I talking rationally . . . skip the french paper I've got to get out of this room this typewriter and find out no . . . I'm okay.

I think I just passed the acid test, I passed through an absolute web of complexities involving the person who had posed the greatest threat and did so with what came close to serenity . . . I wasn't dead (as John later tried to suggest in a veiled form of attack) . . . I liked the music and the coffee and the people and the perfume and the women but I wasn't upset! I wasn't driven back against that wall of incriminations self-accusations self doubts etc. that used to clutter up my people encounters. It went like this:

John* and I were talking on the usual subjects of identity and function in life (he talks so beautifully one would never guess!) I was attacking him as the symbolic beatnik the person who has given free reign to his unconscious who refuses to live a structured existence and identifying him with his brother-in-law Richard who did so badly by his sister etc. I can't do John I haven't even begun to do myself . . . suffice it to say he got back to his high school experience which represents for him a dangerous but exciting search for identity in others, various attempts to graft himself onto more stable environments (that's where he picked up the business about the Jewish home . . . boy did that bug me when he first came out with it!)

---

*John is another friend with whom David spends some time during the period of the diary. He becomes concerned about the possibility of homosexual attraction to John.

My resistances must have been immense because now I remember that night he got drunk he said straight out that he was trying to seduce me (intellectually of course.) Lastly, he keeps wanting to tell me what REALLY is the story between me and Laura and I keep stopping him short . . . I'm still shaky, but less so. When I left him he looked sad. I can't help him and he certainly can't help me . . . I wonder if I can get away from him without feeling like I'm running scared. I must never feel scared again. I must never again feel as if I'm swimming uphill against life. I'm going to sit at this machine until morning if need be . . . until next year . . . (no, until next morning because I've got to see Laura tomorrow) taking things topic by topic, systematizing, ordering, making as little or as much headway as I can. There must be an end and in any case, I have reassured myself that I won't go mad trying. Besides, I didn't dream at all (or probably, the repressant mechanism is healthy again . . . all this is symbolic language who knows what really happens who cares . . . I'm getting better . . . I was close to being sick. Very close. When I finally got to sleep this afternoon).

I have been leafing through Jones on Freud again (I shouldn't . . . I can and should do this on my own maybe I should? What am I afraid of finding out?) I will and it was a positively thrilling discovery that Freud's feelings of greatest worthlessness, as evidenced in his letters, came just prior to his greatest discoveries. But that went on all his life . . . will mine? who cares . . . Freud lived on, riddled with cancer thru a world falling apart with his religion being exterminated exiled from his own country and he kept working . . . he still knew what he had

to do . . . that's what counts . . . that much optimism
and you don't need much else . . . or do you? Have
religions and books and castles been built as mere
excuses? No . . . They mean something but you
don't have to flagellate yourself to know what they
mean as, precisely, the beatnik tenet would say . . .
you can do them and dig them and do and dig yourself all at the same time like a great big ninety ring
circus . . . that's what it means the act of living . . .
the act not the significance of life is real . . . more
real anyway. holy cow it's a jigsaw puzzle and it all
falls together and lord human beings are big big
animals! My hands are literally shaking with excitement . . . this is all so new so new . . . just like they
say why why why does nobody believe them? It's
like a dam that builds and builds and fills up behind with dark things that putrefy and finally something or someone (I must see Laura if only to thank
her) pulls the cork and out it comes gushing and
making a terrible mess and leaving you shaking and
cleaner I want to stay up all night and shine with
cleanliness when I see her tomorrow . . . can I take
it? Is it too soon? . . . no I have to go on living this
isn't a monomania it's just a rebirth, that's all . . . a
mere rebirth.

   You go in and out deeper and shallower and you
come back you always come back it's like a drug but
without the excuse of being drugged drugs do do
that they make you think you're going to know
yourself and then make you forget yourself so they
promise and then they take away promise and take
away someone promised and took her the bitch
Laura my mother my mother promised to love me
and then took it away and gave it back to him and
kept doing that taking it away and giving it back to

him you can't trust them they're not to be trusted
they give and then take back and they make you cry
and leave you frightened and crying and watching
from your crib as they walk away walk away back to
their room bedroom her room they don't rock you
anymore they always stop rocking you and leave
you there in the dark to cry and cry and cry boy I
must have cried like hell as a baby . . . my mother
said I cried a lot . . . post nasal drip or something
she said, the bitch she was lying I knew what they
were doing she was covering up hiding it from me
she was scared and guilty about it and I knew and
cried coming out . . . I'm trembling also smoking a
lot cause it hurts it hurts to know this but I MUST
MUST MUST know this I don't want any more secrets I've had enough secrets secrets kept me from
my beautiful lovely Laura in the purple velvet dress
no more secrets cause of that bitch my mother whip
out the happiness kit its your key your safety valve
your proof it can be done you did it you saw that
morning sometime that morning when it rained
stars it will rain stars again no question about it so I
figured I'd do it to my sister to get him back cause he
liked my sister too come to think of it I kind of did it
with my mother with her her her (oh go on say it
we'll burn the thing) with her panties a fetish that's
all it was no it wasn't. Like my grandfather said my
penis would fall off if I played with it so I played
with it and played with it and am still playing with
it and I suppose I'm still waiting for it to fall off . . .
suppose who are you kidding buster . . . you want it
to fall off want it to wish it would you hate it because because because it did all those things what
things things with mother and father and freddie
and sister and brother that's enough.

Saturday, March 14, 11 A.M.

Everything now conspires to my cure, my whole
body aches to be better (slips of the typewriter . . . is
that possible?) I hadn't realized how sick I was . . .
the bloody stools or at least my queer satisfaction
with them was in my head . . . or libido or whatever
one calls that amazing thing! I awoke after four
hours sleep so as to continue . . . went to take a
shower, brought along vitamin pills (after all I
don't want to die physically in the process of living
emotionally) joked into the mirror saying automatically "Swallowing a bitter pill, eh?" And then, instead of leaving the pills on the tray over the sink I
went right into the shower with them clutched in
my hand . . . I can't stop now . . . and didn't realize
until I was standing there staring at them in amazement (absent mindedness and what I do under it is
another subject for analysis . . . absent mindedness
was on a terrifying increase just prior to the Day)
. . . Falling sleep last night a thousand million
thoughts bubbled then the number the age 18 what
happened when I was 18? (my stomach hurts . . . it
really physically does . . . that blue bear has all
kinds of tricks . . . I'm going out for coffee) Well I
DO have to go out to get some money but I MUST
be merciless with the blue bear. He has no quarter
for me . . . he keeps asking too much demanding too
much (my father kept asking too much love of me
more than I could show him because my mother
would have beaten me what a funny reversal of roles
come to think of it that is about what I was going to
do) in any case it threw up tests too hard to meet I've
recently said that if I can't commit myself both to
marry Laura and to apply immediately to med
school then I'm no good . . . I know I can't meet

tests like that just yet and that creates anxiety, self punishment . . . I had a bad moment when the money Nathan promised to send didn't come (knew rationally that I could get a blank check had money in the bank could charge at the Co-op.) I felt the old surge of hatred as I had against my father this last summer in Europe when money didn't come . . . when love didn't come . . . Everyone knows or accepts by now that such things "the jargon" homosexual conflicts etc. are within them . . . everyone knows that what they do every day has something to do with that jargon, but very few are willing to find out EXACTLY what the connecting links are, what the psychic energy has to do with its product . . . most don't have to until they are shown by some disaster that what they do is foolish, or harmful or too painful for themselves to bear and only then do they ask themselves what those connecting links are, HOW EXACTLY they have been exteriorizing . . . John is driving me crazy (scaring me, still threatening) I called to get that lift down to New York I stumbled on some word (inside myself, still inside myself) and he jumped on it said "Do you feel guilty about something, daddy?" for himself he meant guilty about trying to escape him last night, refusing to let him bother me . . . whatever he meant by Daddy is his problem I suppose the guy you want to make love to has to resemble your father. It's just too uncanny having him take me down to try and come to terms with Laura I had a fear a while back that something inside him would make us crash and although objectively that may yet be my own fear comes from a desire that that should be so, that I should go no further with this analysis but instead give myself up to him as he desires (desires

. . . desires . . . there's another word I used in that letter to Nathan) . . . Acquiesce to my desires I want to beat (love) you that damn letter was in part a love letter . . . (No no it can't be that just stated them in their undeniable form so that I had to face it both the wish to beat and love my father and the wish to love healthily, heterosexually) I mustn't shake John's grip if I'm going to ride in the same car with him that's silly you have to go pretty far to kill yourself even subconsciously directed because you are threatened he probably believes there are plenty of others besides me the fact is I MUST shake John's grip on myself and not scare myself with eery consequences . . . the newspaper odds are AGAINST automobile deaths, that was the resistance mechanism trying to stop me again I'm hot on your tail blue bear that doesn't mean anything what does that mean it means that I'm feeling the denied homosexual instincts, feeling the woman in me and getting over her that's it that's what Faulkner's bear was a woman I have the quotes up on my wall I wrote them down a week ago . . . woman is a bear you must kill the bear to be a man no that isn't what I've got on my wall the quotes go "Anyone could be upset by his first lion."

Comment

This document describes the inner experience of a sensitive, articulate individual in the throes of a serious personal crisis. Although there appear to have been multiple pressures (impending graduation, choice of vocation), the timing of this crisis was apparently determined in part by an event which David construed as evidence that he had been rejected by his girlfriend. In addition he felt betrayed by Nathan, a friend who had sympathized with Laura. The content of the account deals extensively with the theme of rejection. Such an event is hardly a novelty in the life of a young man, so David was apparently uniquely sensitive to it. The extent of his fury and desperation are impressive. Although the document itself does not furnish extensive information about the origin of David's vulnerability to rejection, there are some suggestions. For instance, at one point in the account he writes ". . . so they promise and they take away promise and take away someone promised and took her the bitch Laura my mother my mother promised to love me and then took it away . . . etc." Here Laura and his mother seem joined in common indictment, that they have both promised to love and have broken that promise. We cannot be sure how David might have come to see his mother's caring as unreliable. Perhaps because he had witnessed the frequent fights and reconciliations between his parents, possibly because he too had as a young boy experienced her care for him as capricious and undependable. We simply cannot be sure, and treatment with David would certainly have to be directed in part toward clarifying his relationship with his mother and its patterning effect upon his attitude toward girls he would try to love. At any rate his vulnerability in this area and his experience with Laura interact synergistically at a certain point in David's development. Another contributing theme to the timing of this psychotic episode is related to David's sense that he is being "tested" at this time beyond his capacities. He writes:

> but I must be merciless with the blue bear. He has no quarter for me . . . he keeps asking too much demanding too much (my father kept asking too much love of me more than I could show him because my mother would have

beaten me what a funny reversal of roles come
to think of it that is about what I was going to
do) in any case it threw up tests too hard to
meet I've recently said that if I can't commit
myself both to marry Laura and to apply immediately to med school then I'm no good . . . I
know I can't meet tests like that just yet and
that creates anxiety, self-punishment.

The psychotic episode thus can be seen as an event
which transpires *when* David's life is at an impasse,
when personal development and inner liabilities interact
to stymie him. Treatment of such conditions almost invariably involves measures to remove some of this kind
of pressure. Vocational decisions, plans to leave home,
etc., must often be delayed and approached more
gradually.

Another characteristic of the content of psychotic
states which is variously depicted in individual accounts
is the sense within the subject that the experience is ultimately purposive and is related in a substantive way to
psychological growth. In the present case, one can see
this patient wrestling with those life tasks he has been
called upon to master but has not. Faced with graduation and a career choice which would identify him with
his unhappy father, overwhelmed by failure and guilt in
a sexual relationship, and plagued by a conflict-laden
family environment he must learn to leave, this man sits
down to set in order in a few days a young lifetime of
difficult challenges. He seems curiously drawn to the task
as if he felt that adequate resolution of it would result in
significant inner growth. It is as if something were forcing a number of issues at this stage of his life, and he
seems to have well in mind—even if they are hopelessly
entangled—the principal people involved in these
issues.

This account also illustrates some of the formal characteristics of psychotic states that were described in the previous chapter. For example, this account is characterized primarily by a "psychedelic" altered consciousness. In reading it we obtain a feeling for the way that his experince is inundated with thoughts while being driven toward resolution. Of particular note are the affective shifts which he experiences. Periodically he seems to sense a kind of illumination which temporarily sets his mounting anxiety aside, as when he writes, "I'm out! I'm through . . . boomed out of the tunnel sometime last night and it's raining stars." or "I could be simply overawed but in rereading this I see an incredible, an astonishing structure . . . automatic writing but there is development, there is almost an internal plot . . ." At other times he is floundering at the nadir of despair: "I can't cope, I can't come to grips . . . it's Hawthorne's disease blazing away, red guilt or little stringy black warts . . . ." The formal characteristic of rapidly shifting cognitive grasp and emotional tone will be apparent in many of the accounts that will be presented. The flood of new or unfamiliar material into consciousness forces attempts at heroic coping and compels explanation. We may reasonably wonder what the significance of this new material is. For instance, in the present account, what is the significance of David's question about his possible homosexuality toward the end of the diary? Do we regard the emergence of such specific concerns as clear-cut evidence that these very conflicts are crucially involved in precipitating the current psychopathological state? Young men in the throes of a psychotic reaction often develop concerns about homosexuality or fears that they may be feminine. Does this mean that the essential conflict in such individuals has to do with homosexuality or, by contrast, is it likely that a host of incompletely

resolved developmental issues may be thrust into consciousness during an acute psychosis? We recall that
Freud formulated an entire theory of paranoid psychosis
based upon Schreber's ideation concerning sexual identity during his psychotic illness. In essence, we might ask
in this instance whether the psychosis was a manifestation of homosexual conflicts or whether it was the other
way around. Does fragmentation of the mental self-representation produce a strikingly repetitious phenomenology? It seems likely that the psychotic state, like the
dream, is a permissive state which allows for a number of
alterations in consciousness. It is our contention that
psychotic altered states of consciousness are characterized by relatively novel ways of perceiving and equally
surprising percepts. One might well expect that the phenomenology of psychotic consciousness would be subject to the same distortions of latent meaning as is the
manifest content of dreams. (See Freud's conjecture on
this point quoted in the *Introduction.*) Great care must
be taken in assigning controlling dynamic significance
to any one percept. Such considerations are important in
the treatment of psychotic states and we will have more
to say about them in subsequent sections of this book.

3. *Psychosis Associated with the Use of Antidepressant Medication in the Context of Heterosexual Rejection*

CRAIG

Craig was a 19-year-old student who had dropped out of his first year of college at the beginning of the second semester because of depression and progressive inability to concentrate on his courses. Upon leaving school he began outpatient psychiatric treatment and was placed on antidepressant medication (tricyclic compound). Some three weeks later he began to be increasingly restless and anxious, and to suffer from progressive insomnia. These symptoms gave way to feelings of having "waked up" and "become alive," ideas that rapidly assumed an exaggerated and delusional quality. He was hospitalized and the working diagnosis was acute schizophrenia. Craig's life had suffered its first significant blow when he was only 11 years old. At this time his mother, with whom he had a particularly close—if not exclusive—relationship, died as a result of malignant melanoma. The boy then went to live with his maternal grandmother until his father remarried two years later.

79

Two and one-half years before admission to the hospital, the grandmother also died. Despite his early enforced dependence upon his father, Craig had been unable to develop a close relationship with him and this fact had been a source of profound conflict and disappointment. Approximately a year and one-half before admission, however, he fell deeply in love for the first time and was happy and confident until this relationship terminated approximately nine months later. It was at this point that he attempted to begin college but was overcome at the end of one semester by serious depressive feelings which led to three suicide attempts resulting in his subsequent withdrawal from school and his beginning psychiatric treatment.

Following his admission to the hospital, Craig was treated with antipsychotic drugs which rapidly diminished his anxiety and brought his referential ideas under control. During this early aftermath, approximately three weeks after admission, he wrote the following unsolicited account in the stream-of-consciousness style which has been preserved here. In addition, his periodic use of capital letters for emphasis has been retained. Names have been altered to protect the anonymity of the patient and his family. Tragically, this patient committed suicide while on pass before he had been discharged from the hospital.

TITLE: A DAY, A NIGHT, AND
MORE DEDICATED TO ANYONE

Part One: Problems
   Antisocial problems. Picking my nose. Homosexuality, unstable relationship with my father, lack of communication between father and self. The force

of my mother's death. Dependence between father and self. Honesty, sincerity, TRUTH. Afraid that girlfriends will die, like mother: of cancer, insecure. Identified quite a bit with my mother. The truth about myself is hardest to face. Relationship between artists and homosexuality—I am a big hypochondriac, weak relationship with father, suicidal tendencies. Now I am concerned about my relationship with my father. Leads up to thoughts of homosexuality. Paranoid (no trust), schizoid, masochism. Broken relationship with girlfriend. Demand perfection from myself. Problems of self control. He wasn't a boy, only a man. He wasn't a man, only a boy. On awakening, a baby, a slow awakening, a downhill period followed by a burst of energy. My mother's death left me with great feelings of insecurity. One of the effects has been that I either want a strong (and immediate) relationship with a girl or none at all. The thought of homosexuality does not upset me today (as much) since my relationship with my father has improved so much lately. We've still got a long way to go, but it's worth it to me and worth the effort and worth the time and worth the everything and worth my father (most of all). I would like to sing. I would like to live most of all. I would like to write. YES! Why? I don't know whether I should go to sleep or stay awake. It's bad to depend too much on anyone or anything: a girl—or ANYTHING! We all pay for the mistakes we make. Eventually and here on earth. Yellow-sun. Brown-dirt. Blue-sky, sea blue feelings. Greengrass, nature. Red-fiery passion, love. Black-death, night. White-purity, daytime (and morning a new life commences). A new world awakens. My life seems unreal. A scene badly written in which I must play. A breath of fresh air, in the morning. Why is everyone (including myself) afraid of dying and death? Even dying is a creative act? I am paranoid when it comes to laws which I must obey and other commands which I am forced (by myself) to follow. I depend entirely too much on music. Buy why? I get too wound up in the songs. Is this bad? No, not if it is a controlled response of emotions within your gut. At last I am gaining back my respect for my father; a respect which had vanished for the last eighteen months. He respects me too, I think. I'm afraid that old illnesses and bad ideas might come to the surface again and explode. I'm afraid that I may be in the ward forever. I don't trust other people as I should. Live and luck. Great luck. I feel an acute shortage of exercise. I wish that I could run, leap and frolic like other kids. My mother's death was a traumatic experience for me. Ever since then I've been afraid that I might be left alone. I feel guilty and greatly insecure all the time despite the ridiculousness of it all. The world is not in chaos, it's just an example of much confusion—and mass confusion. I'm still afraid that I may commit suicide or give up here. I have little confidence in myself. I'm also afraid that I may be committed to a long-term hospitalization. (What a tongue twister, for students of English). I am a terrible hypochondriac and I do it for attention. I still have self-pity, which is bad. That's bad. I know my father is plugging away for me for the first time in a long, long while. I try to avoid my own problems by focusing on the problems of other people. Why can't I face them? I am insecure, afraid that my girlfriends may die suddenly like my mother. I'm a perfectionist—too much guilt, too much fear too.

Sense of inferiority, inadequacy. IMPATIENCE, INSECURITY, Condescending. My identity: me-dad, me-girlfriend, now me-me I hope so. Love versus hatred. Unsecurity, perfection, creativity, hypochondriac, identity. Before: totally identified with father, wanted to kill him by killing myself, wanted to kill a girl by killing myself. Illnesses are all psychosomatic mostly including melanoma (which my mother died of). Fear of God, an angry God, a jealous God, a negative God. When you are positive then you are really truly happy. Pain has an element of black, pain has an element of blank. Not a compassionate God, not an understanding God, not a sympathetic God. Not a compassionate father, not an understanding father, not a sympathetic father. My view of God is more reasonable than my father's. Guidance instills fear. AFRAID.

Part Two: Clearing Things Up

The lovely robin is the harbinger of spring. After you wake up there are many dawning decisions to be made—and later too. Dawn is but a rising star, dusk is but a falling star. He walked over to see her, but she snubbed him and he cried about it later and he died later also. I am but a shooting star or a comet or a body revolving around the earth which in turn also revolves around the sun and I am happy. Are you? Delusions frighten every one, including you—and me. Am I sick? Do I look it or deserve to be? Do you think so? Well, I don't. Not really. "If most people were to be born twice they'd probably call it dying"—e.e. cummings. I write whatever thoughts emerge from the crossroads of my mind, brain. Kicks are just getting harder to find. I remember her eyes: soft, dark, and brown. Said she had never been in trouble—not even in town (which is a good thing). In a few more days they'll call us right for each other. One of those girls that seems to come in the spring. To feel you all around me and take your hand along the sand. Catch the wind, kill my fears. Swift fingers reaching out into the pockets of my mind. Let me settle slowly, not fast. I just met a good-looking girl. She was wearing a white turtleneck and looked really hot. My note to you: my nose has been bothering me. It is a reality and I wouldn't have revealed this secret except for the fact that I am aiming at the truth. STOP! NOW! For the past few days I have acted like a hypochondriac, idiot, fool. I have had bad delusions that my nose (my left nostril) was bleeding. It doesn't matter. It was stupid to start with in the beginning. I am compiling thoughts for this day, this life, this world, the end. I just had breakfast, nothing special, just pastries. I am not tired even though it is 9:13 in the morning. Say you love me too . . . please! Faces are funny and faces are sad. Handsome person, ugly, bad mood. I look happy now. I look ugly now, at this instant. There is too much hatred, jealousy and envy in this world and in all bad things in this world. Crazy people aren't really crazy: they're only just screwed-up, dislocated, angry, fouled up emotionally disturbed PEOPLE. Nothing to worry about at all. My brain is running out of thoughts. I am panicking. I am afraid that I won't have anything to say when I come back to my work which isn't really work but only a pleasureable experience (and my pad of paper and my redinked pen which I am manipulating now in order to freeze my thoughts forever, and let them out of inside). There are tracks across and all over my brain, the tracks of lost memories and fleeting, transient, eroding, disappearing, lost, undiscovered, uncovered memories. I am SAD that I could not fully express my feelings and uncover them. I am in *this* ward in *this* hospital, New England, eastern U.S.A., Western Hemisphere, North of the equator, earth sun's solar system, further away than Mercury, but not nearly as out of it as Pluto, Neptune, Uranus, Saturn, Jupiter, Venus or Mars. This is my address, each planet is unique unto itself. So AM I and you. I'm sad and I am stuck (like mud) in this here ward. But I'm happy at the same time instantly. I am listening to records as I quite often do. I also just went through the ritual which is done fourteen times a day of taking medication. The end. The windows in this room were just cleaned. It took a lot of effort and work on someone's time to do this. Boy were they dirty before, not now, better. I can see again. I am getting a delusion now. I am afraid that some one will take this pad (my manuscript) away from me and exterminate it and me forever because of jealousy. Exterminate fear! PLEASE! I am frightened, obsessed, and fractured by the preceding thought. It is irrational (totally, but not entirely). I walk around, armed with common sense. I am delusional, afraid that someone will insist on this being read now. I would be mad and become irrational. I am just experimenting, nothing more. I'm not trying to hurt anyone. PLEASE UNDERSTAND PLEASE! Oh. God, I woke up about six this morning, the sun was shining. I am still very unstable, extremely. I feel like Abraham Lincoln (except that I have no beard). It's the way that I hold my sports jacket with my hands. Very stoutfully in front of myself. It's just past lunch, don't feel so good, too much eating. I'm lonely and sad. I'm lonely and sad. I wish I had my girl (even *a* girl) with me. There is one special person: it's nothing serious yet and I could take it if we broke up, but (if we have it my way) I'll marry her if necessary or something like that. I am not writing for money. But rather I am seeking to find my own sense of identity and become independent. So badly that it hurts! I am phony in a lot of ways. Unfortunately I know that Sadness has an element of pain and an element of blank. You only have eyes for the one you love so badly, so madly. SENSITIVITY has a strange element of realism. It's only skin deep but it's so familiar to us, all too familiar. After you break up you wonder . . . WHY? WHY? WHY?

Part Three: Recovery

I saw a shadow touch a shadow's hand. Nobody said life is fair. There is a time for everything (living, dying), the right time is harder to find. How can you break a marshmallow? Void, a void (avoid voids) . . . the sin of love's false security. Go away from my window, leave at your own chosen speed. I am not the one you want, I am not the one you need, it ain't me you're looking for, babe. The hypnotic—splattered mist was lifting (slowly). Ben Franklin's "Bold and Arduous Plan for Arriving at Moral Perfection" . . . Walden is great, really, Thoreau must be respected for his individuality. Thoreau must also be admired for his simplicity at Walden Pond. My writing is getting phony, I refuse to continue under false circumstances. My mind (like a blanket) holds no ideas or convictions. Give me a chance. . . The only truth I know is you, If I had never loved I never would have cried. In the deserts of the heart let the healing fountains start. An INFINITELY GENTLE, infinitely SUFFER-ING THING. Time is a tree (one life, one leaf). But love is the sky and I am for you. Fear (at end) of death. Dying doesn't hurt, it only knocks the hell out of you. It rips the soul into too many, a lot of little pieces. I was frightened. I said, Marie, Marie, hold ME tight. She did. Moody blue to-day. I've been thinking, me: Jesus Christ, dad: God—pinned and wriggling on the cross. There's lots more living to do before this story is ended (of my life). For every mile the feet go, the heart goes nine. I talkingly stepped out the door. The fog that was there screamed at me loudly. Shut up it said. There's a GROOVY THING GOIN' NOW IT'S CALLED SEX.

Comment

This account, covering a period of several days, was written by a young man soon after admission to the hospital with an acute psychotic reaction. At the outset, we should mention several points regarding the authenticity of the account. This young man obviously felt that setting his thoughts down on paper made sense for him. He enjoyed literary subjects in general and writing in particular, and may have even hoped that someday writing would be part of his vocation. We would hypothesize, however, that his experience is not unique, but rather, in its formal aspects, rather characteristic of the early period following hospitalization for many psychotic patients. His verbal ability may have made it possible for him to communicate—however imperfectly—an extremely complex experiential state which other patients live through but are unable to articulate. Secondly, one might ask whether he really meant what he wrote. Do some of the apparently trivial or sentimental passages mean that he was not serious in his undertaking or that his expressions of emotion were superficial or feigned? Probably not. On the contrary, it is likely that he was earnestly attempting to put down what he was experiencing. Tragic, though in support of this contention, is the fact of his later suicide. Thus, I am assuming that this is an authentic document. Certain aspects of its form and content require further comment with regard to our attempt to understand the determinants of the experiential ingredients of the acute psychosis.

The timing of this psychotic episode is similar to that of the first record presented (David). The end of a heterosexual relationship apparently was a triggering event in Craig's life, occurring within a life experience already sensitized to abandonment by the untimely death of both mother and grandmother. Another ingredient was probably important in determining the timing of this episode, however. Antidepressant drug administration appears to have been temporally related to the onset of this psychotic event. Certain types of drugs appear capable of initiating a psychotic state in certain individuals, resulting in a weakening of defensive mechanisms which may have previously contained specific intrapsychic conflicts.

Apparently, the form of this young man's inner experience was extremely complex during the period covered by this account. He was simultaneously being assailed by a host of sensations and ideas. ("There are tracks across and all over my brain, the tracks of lost memories and fleeting, transient, eroding, disappearing, lost, undiscovered, uncovered memories.") Thus, his altered consciousness is characterized in part by a sense of hypermnesis, the experience that memories, long forgotten, are returning with great rapidity and force. The memories are probably selective and conform to rather specific content themes, particularly those of loneliness, maternal abandonment, and guilt. Another aspect of his altered state is the representation of growth strivings in consciousness. Despite his extraordinary vulnerability ("on awakening, a baby, a very slow awakening. . ."), he has not abandoned the challenges of continued growth ("We've still got a long way to go, but it's worth it to me . . ."). He strives for order and structure throughout the account and attempts to begin by locating himself quite concretely, however facetiously he may have intended it ("I am here in *this* ward, in *this* hospital, New England, eastern U.S.A., Western Hemisphere. . ." etc.). Then there is a self-conscious grasping for the rudiments of self-definition, and he seems only too aware of the tentative and relatively inauthentic status of his thoughts in this regard ("My identity: me-dad, me-girlfriend, now me-me. I hope so. . . But rather I am seeking to find my own sense of identity and become independent. So badly that it hurts!") Facing the deficits in himself and his own life experience thus far, he is extremely self-critical ("The truth about myself is hardest to face. . . . I am a terrible hypochondriac and I do it for attention . . . It was stupid to start with in the beginning . . . I look ugly now, at this instant. . . I'm a phony in a lot of ways."). The account is, therefore, a curious and tortuous combination of aspiration and self-depreciation, of self-defined assets and deficits. This "balance-sheet" kind of self-experience is further being lived here in the context of a highly compressed, distilled, and telescoped inner conception of the time required for psychological growth.

With regard to content, the sudden, shattering loss of maternal anchoring and support which Craig had experienced at his mother's untimely death had somehow

been relived during the unsuccessful love affair. ("Afraid
that girlfriends will die, like mother: of cancer, insecure.") This theme saturates the entire account. On the
one hand he is bereft, and on the other, he is filled with
rage at those who have caused him such pain (". . .
wanted to kill a girl by killing myself"). The helplessness in the face of real and symbolic maternal abandonment is apparently experienced as a threat to bodily
integrity and to life itself. ("I'm afraid that old illnesses
and bad ideas might come to the surface again and explode. . . . I'm still afraid that I may commit suicide or
give up here.") On the other hand, movement toward an
adult male orientation is seriously hampered by his impression of his father as distant, malign, and unsupport-
ive. ("Not a compassionate God, not an understanding
God, not a sympathetic God. Not a compassionate father, not an understanding father, not a sympathetic
father.")

In summary, this individual's inner experience is
characterized by competing simultaneous themes of (1)
anger, fear and nostalgia at being abandoned by maternal figures while being abruptly thrust into early adulthood; (2) desire for psychological growth, yet fear of
adult male identification in the person of his father; (3)
intense impatience and self-criticism and the pervading
sense that resolution between these conflicting motives is
both urgent and impossible. It is not difficult, given this
form of inner experience, to account for certain consequences such as hopeless immobilization, despair, or
suicide. From the point of view of treatment, awareness
of this inner state can provide a beginning framework
for the establishment of a therapeutic relationship. A
therapist must, first of all, acknowledge and stress the
authenticity of the patient's dilemma. He must show the
patient that he is aware of the difficulty involved in aban-

doning the regressive wish to give up in the struggle for psychological growth. On the other hand, he must work to assist the patient to remove some of the unrealistic, self-imposed demands that growth occur too rapidly. Finally, he must help the patient define an adult role model which is a corrective alternative to those which the patient has previously envisaged.

4. Psychosis Associated with Adolescent Psychosexual Development

RUSSELL

Subjective experience in acute psychosis is characterized by varying degrees and forms of acknowledgment of conflict. This next account is noteworthy for its open recognition of personal inadequacy and—though somewhat verbose—is frankly and rather realistically confessional. This 20-year-old college student, who was hospitalized very briefly for a stormy, self-limited psychotic episode, was an intelligent young man, who had always taken great pride in his academic and rational abilities. A "loner" much of his youth, his intellectual life was considerably more developed than his social or emotional life. He regarded himself as unattractive and particularly unappealing to women. The increasing academic and social pressures of college led to a crisis in his own development, which he described in a personal interpretation of his struggle written prior to hospitalization. The words italicized for emphasis are his own.

The Natural Sciences, carried ever onward, pose no threat. The Socratic "Why" must never be asked to our own lives. "Why live?" is the loudest of all questions for there is no answer. To fight, to help others? The *why's* transcend our experience and we cannot give an answer. Thus when we ask of the cause of life *we get no answer!* We discover, to the limits of both our knowledge and our knowledge-ability, simply blind causes and nothing else.

To my parents: I have been recently inquiring into the meaning of life. As you know, I am a mechanist and am not impressed with transcendent ideals such as God and duty. Thus, I am a complete materialist. I have believed for some time that happiness is the purpose for life. I have examined human and animal behavior and found that there are similarities. Thus I dissect my own and other people's motives according to those laws. This morning I was considering these things which I had known for some time. I saw clearly that life has no meaning, life just *is*. It occurred to me that if this were so why didn't I kill myself. And I saw that there was no reason. This is not a fit of depression. It is the final scrutiny of reason by itself. It is not an emotional problem and must not be treated as such. My only hope is that I forget. The best way for this that I can see is forgetfulness which can be provided by hypnosis. I must be "programmed" never to come down this path again. I am also writing a note to my philosophy professor. I discussed my viewpoints with him before I realized the horror they entailed. Talk with him; he will understand my problem and the nature of my terrible, new-found knowledge. Remember: my only salvation lies in forgetfulness.

To my philosophy professor: I am not in despair about the impossibility of morality; on the contrary

I had been ecstatic over my vanquishment of these transcendental cobwebs. It was when I realized that my awful knowledge showed there was no scientific ground of being, that life just happened, and that from now on all my possible pleasures, contentments, and joys would would be forever vacuous, seen by myself as the S ⟶ R activities of a meaningless insect on a meaningless planet in a meaningless universe. Man requires either a transcendental end or none, his eyes must see beyond existence or he must have no memory. He must have either no memory, live for immediate impulses or he must have faith in life's unreality, of the existence of the transcendental universe to hide from his eyes the horror of life. I keep saying *horror* but no word can explain this ultimate despair, the terrible knowledge of the nothingness of life. Do not seek to show me a fault in my reasoning; it is true! if you fail, you will give me only misery and you may catch this monstrous infection from me. Turn your gaze outward not inward. Just as a society is sapped of its vitality as soon as its meaningless reasons for existence are laid before it, so must the individual. Perhaps you, not being a reductionist like myself, can contemplate my thoughts without finding the vacuum which I have found.

To my parents: I cannot bear what I have uncovered. It is not an emotional collapse. It is due to the sublimation of the will to act into pure thoughts. It is due not to depression but to knowledge—pure, abstract. Knowledge in whose terrible light the will to live must wither and die. Terrible knowledge. I can seek my peace only in extinction or forgetfulness.

What is life in which all values, all pleasures are dissected and laid bare by the sweet light of reason. It is horror! Please do not allow me to be again until I have been told to forget this. This cannot be treated in the normal psychiatric manner—uncover the seat of the patient's disturbance, discover it to him, and help him to face it. By my insistent prodding, pushed on by my insatiable thirst for self knowledge finally uncovered it this morning. The horror is such that I cannot, will not, bear it. Do not force me to do so. At last I have found the truth and I wither in its awful light. It is the very negation of my existence.

Do not seek to trace the tracks which my mind traveled lest you too become infected. Seek, rather, to destroy those tracks in my own mind and save me, for if I am not given oblivion of my memory then I shall have the oblivion of my mind. When you make over my mind, as you must, please don't give me faith or altruism or some other such filth. Give me instead a clear distrust of self-introspection, of psychoanalyzing others. Give me a healthy unease at these people who seek to puzzle our human life and lay it bare before us. Not that they are wrong! On the contrary, they are right and they must stop seeking the cause, the reason for our minds or they will destroy us all as I have been destroyed by my own folly. I am like Oedipus Rex, the man who had to know and whose awful knowledge forced him to destroy himself. I must stay active, for when I cease to act I must *be*, a horror which I cannot now allow. You think perhaps that my breakdown is due to my tendency to over-scientize things too much. You are so right! Not because of the confusions which it breeds but because of the truth it inspires, that unnameable, abominable truth which destroys all men who behold it with the nothingness of its horrid, unholy light. Know thyself—destroy thyself. You will destroy life if you explain it, if you put its wonderful properties on a scale. How often I have heard this sentence from my friends and how often I laughed at their fears and talked of the wonders to come when our motives were objectively explained, when our "animal instincts" were conquered, and we would enter a utopia. How right they were and how deep was my folly. How I wish that I was now anywhere than where I am now, for I would have retained my identity which I have now lost. My initial treatment should be fairly simple. I should be hypnotized and told to forget the last few days. I should be told never to travel again the paths that led me to this simple but ghastly conclusion: they are this. Kant says that duty, to be autonomous (free) the will must concentrate on a transcendental end or else we must choose our actions in response to the demands of causality. But this can't be. (Don't ask me how, don't even think about it). Therefore there are no morals. Now, having explained everything except the meaning of life, which has no reason, I despair of life and of happiness. My great will to know, my scientific mentality, my insatiable thirst; these are precious, are they not? No! They are a curse. They must be squelched.

I must keep writing until the sedative puts me out lest my thoughts should turn upon myself and I be forced to gaze upon the mindless, soul-eating horror which I have discovered. It is nothing supernatural or outside of myself. It is simply that I shall never be able to enjoy my life. My happiness, my values will be looked upon as transient and arbitrary, my pleasures as fleeting impulses. Each will be analyzed in detail, dissected and thus killed. What can I do in the face of such negation of the true nature of life. Life isn't moved by some outside purpose; it simply *is*. We must not seek purpose for it has none. Even now, it is not because of this horror that I wish to close my eyes. It is the fact that my knowledge is the negation of life; they cannot coexist. Either the knowledge or life must be destroyed and since I prefer not to die, I must have this pernicious memory removed. My reason must be reduced to simply a tool. I must be motivated by my noblest instincts—not faith, altruism, or other such drivel but my pride (what little there is), my inventiveness (through its will toward myself and toward the study of life, more psych than bio), my fairness toward others, my desire to dominate nature over other men.

To myself: If you survive you will have forgotten why you wrote this. You uncovered the meaning of life and discovered a horror which no human being can bear. Do not seek to reduce the wonderful process of life to its components. If you cut up a cat to see what makes it alive you will have killed it. The same is true of your own life. Seek not self-knowledge.

To anyone: Life has no purpose. Life just is. How often we write this simple sentence but never realize its full impact. The scientific mind seeks everywhere for causes. "causality-seeking" is the definition of the rationalist mind. We have seen in our day the complete scientist. Everything can be reduced to scientific terms. It is true! I have done it. I came to this conclusion long ago. But there are limits to pure reason beyond which the scientist cannot proceed. Included behind this impenetrable veil is the ground of his own being. The limits of pure reason are absolutely, forever impassable. For all minds, scientific and mystic, knowledge cannot transcend those boundaries. Kant tried but failed. How can I, how can any *self* be the object of our will. Within his framework of reality the scientist cannot justify the ground of his own being. His life is meaningless! I am not advocating a return of faith. The sight of weak people justifying their existence as "servants of the Lord" sickens me. Life needs no justification, must have none. Life just is.

To my friends: You were 99% right. Life cannot be defined. Not quite true. It *must not* be defined. I defined and found cosmic horror—an unspeakable vacuum. Don't seek to know yourself. Do not seek, simply *be.* Don't sit on your pedestal and think! Do! I have finished my quest for knowing. It has destroyed me. Take care lest it destroy you. *Facta, non verba.* It is not meaning which justifies life, it is living life itself. Life tends toward self-knowledge but this is only a means. The end is life. Do not define, just live. I know this sounds like some sort of madness or 1930 fantasy story, but it is true! You cannot see how mere knowledge, simple knowledge could blast my soul? Good! Because it did! Do not ask how, do not seek to find the nature of this malady for when you find its nature you will find the greatest of horrors—non-ego, non-being, non-self.

To me: When you read this you will understand if the terror has not left you or you will not understand. My life in all its facets has been an insatiable quest for knowledge. I recognized the highest form of knowledge self-knowledge toward which I strove. Finally I have discovered my self and its purpose. My self is an automaton, my purpose is non-existent.

Comment

It is possible to recognize in this record an expression of concerns commonly encountered in thoughtful adolescents. "The meaning of life" as an intellectual focus during adolescence appropriately parallels rapid refocusing of personal and emotional goals. This process reached an impasse and took on the aspects of a crisis in this young man's life. Intellectualism had long served as a protective shield behind which deeply felt personal insecurity could be hidden from internal and external view. As development proceeded, this shield became less effective in the challenging and demanding college milieu. We were unable to learn in our relatively brief contact with Russell what specific assaults upon his uneven development actually triggered the brief psychotic episode. However, the timing of this event was essentially determined by his going to college, an experience which tests a number of developmental skills, for it requires living and functioning apart from immediate parental support. He must learn to bear loneliness, to seek the companionship and support of peers, and to accept the challenges of an adult sexual role. These obligatory developmental tasks, which must be pursued in the context of a more overt program of intellectual development, comprise the "hidden agenda" of college experience but are no less real for that. When prior development has successfully prepared an individual for these maturational steps, the process of inner growth will continue with manageable stress. If such preparation has been inadequate or skewed, successful articulation of early adolescence with the college experience may be much more problematic.

We were unable to get to know Russell well enough to determine the origins of the personality liabilities he carried into the college milieu; specifically, what intrafamilial forces led to or facilitated the high priority accorded intellectual versus personal and psychological development.

The psychotic altered state in this instance was characterized first of all by rather sudden, incapacitating anxiety and disruption in the experience of self, which is usually not a primary focus of conscious experience. "Do not ask how, do not seek to find the nature of this malady for when you find its nature you will find the greatest of horrors—non-ego, non-being, non-self . . . finally I have discovered my self and its purpose. My self is an automaton, my purpose is non-existent." Another aspect of the form of this experience is the sense that some momentous insight has been achieved, some realization that is life-changing and sufficient to put all the past in an understandable context. This aspect of the experience has the qualities of a "peak" or revelatory episode as described in the first chapter. The surety with which explanation and conviction come at such moments has to be recognized as deriving from the nature of this kind of consciousness, not necessarily from its cognitive content. Critical examination, reflection, and reasoning are suspended, in fact are brushed aside by the power of such an experience.

The content of Russell's conscious struggle is concerned with some sudden disenchantment with an obsessive, analytic approach to life. He seems to be saying that somehow life without feeling and spontaneity is empty and pointless. "Do not define, just live." He perceives with great pain the absence of these ingredients in himself. We would assume that this content is, at some dynamic level, very much determined by the psychological makeup of Russell himself. Some characteristic defenses—particularly the obsessive, self-punitive style of thinking—are quite evident. This is an example of the person-specific content that emerges in the setting of the psychotic altered state of consciousness.

In treatment we were able to acknowledge with him the essential reality of the growth tasks which he perceived and to encourage him to plan some more realistic, prolonged program for the achievement of his goals. His "motivation" we understood in terms of his felt experience of developmental conflict and his strong desire ultimately to resolve that conflict.

ELLEN

The previous documents demonstrate the shifting tolerance which the individual in the early stages of a psychotic reaction can have toward the experience of psychic pain or conflict. Sometimes the relevant psychological issues are perceived quite clearly; more often the psychotic state provides some degree of affective and/or ideational protection from the experience of conflict. Through my own clinical experience I have come to the position that the continuum separating realistic appreciation from illusory mastery of conflict is an important clinical dimension in psychotic states. Frequently the patient's position on this continuum changes as the acute psychotic experience recedes. It is my conviction that monitoring and effecting such change is a crucial task for the therapist in the early weeks of treatment. Sometimes in the accounts which patients write one can obtain some indication of the way the psychotic experience will ultimately be represented intrapsychically.

In this account we have an example of an experience which is nearly completely illusory or "wishful" and essentially completely devoid of conscious awareness of conflict. Ellen was a 24-year-old girl whose social experience had been extremely limited. She had few friends and rarely dated. Following graduation from high school she had obtained work as a cashier in a department store. At one point a man considerably older than she, whose marriage was dissolving, began to give her quite a rush. He asked her for dates and made it clear that he was interested in having intercourse with her. In the context of this dilemma Ellen become psychotic and wrote the following document which began with a series of dates, names, and numbers.

Born 1943—Ellen Dean Relnich $3 + 3 = 6$ $4 + 3 = 7$

1940   Cedrick Simpson Jr. $3 + 3 = 6$ $3 + 3 = 6$ $9 + 4 = 13$

1942   Thomas Chase $4 + 2 = 6$

1959   George Thompson—mad crush in junior high and high school. I loved his large lips for some inconceivable reason, but I never went out with any boys in high school.

1957   Cedrick Simpson met me and liked me at the same time he was thinking of marriage. He was seventeen and I was fourteen at the time he gave me a kiss on the lips.

1963   Graveyard—Lucinda was a name on the gravestone $6 + 3 = 9$

1963   I began dating Thomas Chase.

1964   I took a practical nursing course at hospital. $6 + 4 = 10$ He had an operation for a rupture in the same hospital, because his wife was trying to work him to death.

1964   Thomas Chase—We broke up two months later, he was engaged again seeking seductive love. She was not a virgin when he met her. Cedrick left his wife for good in May and found me in August. I wanted for some inconceivable reason pyrex dishes, silverware sets and towels, also, I wanted the last two weeks in August off. August seventeenth I began my two week vacation. I was seeking something inconceivable the week before, while at work I felt an uncontrollable force explainable only by God. There was miserable weather one week before vacation and one week after vacation. On August eighteenth Cedrick called and asked me to go out. He told me he had to ask me for some reason but I never even thought of falling in love with him. I expressed only apathy for him at that time. We stayed out until one p.m.

August 18, $8 + 1 = 9$, to August 26, $2 + 6 = 8$-miserable weather wet, rainy, cloudy, cold. I got home at two o'clock the twenty-fifth, rainy, cloudy - $2 + 5 = 7$.

August 26, peaceable sleep - $2 + 6 = 8$. I got home at four o'clock and felt a strong euphoria. When I arrived home there was a praying mantis at the door. I didn't think of it at the time as being a set pattern of any kind. On Sunday the 27th he came over to drop off my phonograph. I woke up at seven and had a strange sensation. I had to get out and look at the sky. A warmth of love enslaved my body and soul and I felt that a miracle had enveloped or was soon to occur within a week. Cedrick came and kissed me and he left to pick up his son. I called him and he asked if I wanted to meet his son and I said I wanted to more than anything in the world right now. I saw his beautiful son and felt warmth in my soul and heart for him. That night we went to his brother's house. I wanted to get the Ouija Board. For some reason the signs at that time were many. On the 28th we used the Ouija Board for signs; it told me to go to the Evangelical Lutheran Church at two o'clock. The church was built in 1965. There the reverend thought I had committed a sin and that I was guilty of seductive love. The next day I went to the theater and was experiencing a constant euphoria. At the theater I sat in the seventh row and the eleventh seat.   1 + 1 = 2. The singer sang songs that proved that this miracle was true. Through the understanding of Jesus Christ. A comic talked about sex, and everyone was in hysterics but me. A strange feeling of euphoria came over me and enveloped me. He said that to sum it up girls do not know what love is, that they receive it in the wrong way and that there is no one in the audience that is pure. I moved down to row one, seat five, and a woman pointed out to me the only unreserved seat. It was the first row the seventh seat.   7 + 1 = 8.

As Cedrick and I departed as friends I saw a falling star in the East. Then a pulsating star getting brighter and dimmer then brighter and dimmer. I went to a doctor for a check-up and the doctor could not believe I was a virgin. He said they are so hard to find these days. On August twenty-ninth there were other songs and other clues. One was about dreaming, some one to love me, dreaming that my love would come true. Another song spoke of some-one who was very lonely, another was was "Love

Breaks My Heart But It's Useless to Cry." Tonight I
see shooting stars in space. Something is coming,
there is a clue, maybe tonight. Another song
"Three-Thousand Miles Away" made me think of
June 1964 when my mother and father were separated and I took a long trip with my father. I heard
on the radio an evangelist. He talked about love,
seduction, right men, and right women. He talked
of a house built on sand, will fall; built on rock it
will withstand. Men and women must be faithful to
each other. Maybe tonight just down the block on a
beach something's coming. I don't know what it is
but maybe tonight.

   If and when I find the face of faces, even when
that face smiles then and only then will I know
love.

Comment

   The timing of this psychotic episode was related to a
confrontation with the challenges of adult heterosexual
development. Ellen, who had very little dating experience prior to the episode she described, developed an
acute psychotic reaction in the context of this totally new
experience. It is a repeated clinical observation that acute
psychotic reactions often develop in the context of the
pursuit of an adult sexual role. The developmental preparation required for successful establishment of this role
is extremely complex and lies at the core of human development and the humanizing process. Among the personality strengths prerequisite for satisfactory adaptive
mastery of this task are a desire for and comfort in the
establishment of peer human relationships, a relative
and age-appropriate decrement in infantile, dependent

emotional bonding with parental figures, and a capacity for the reasonable internal modulation of guilt. Many individuals who become psychotic in adolescence are not sufficiently capable in these areas. In Ellen's case, she had a lifelong history of asociality and seemed to have retreated from socializing experiences in early adolescence. Further, she and her mother seemed bound by an emotional tie which precluded Ellen's continuing development toward genuine adulthood. She apparently never participated with parental guidance and support in those myriad incremental steps toward adult sexuality which adolescence demands. This developmental gap which the "affair" asked her to bridge was simply too wide.

The altered consciousness which thus supervened is noteworthy. Once again we encounter the form of consciousness in which revelatory meaning appears close at hand. Throughout Ellen's account there is a preoccupation with numbers; various dates are manipulated in a rather arbitrary way and are reacted to as if they set forth some momentous purpose or design. "I was seeking something inconceivable the week before, while at work I felt an uncontrollable force explainable only by God." The euphoric response, the sense of urgency, of being led, the tendency to notice trivial details, and the press for meaning are formal experiential characteristics of the altered state. Personal dynamic themes and wishes flow into the structure of the altered consciousness and give it unique, individual-specific content.

This content centers around Ellen's conflict between desires for an adult heterosexual relationship, however naively conceived, and her fear of such a relationship. The specific dates which she strings together document her pitiably sparse prior experiences with men. Her loneliness is poignantly represented: "On August twenty-ninth there were other songs and other clues. One was about dreaming, someone to love me, dreaming that my love would come true." Equally in evidence is her anticipated guilt: "He said that to sum it up girls do not know what love is, that they receive it in the wrong way and that there is no one in the audience that is pure." Also characteristic of Ellen is the wishful form of much of her fantasy. In fact this account contains minimal evidence of terror, depression, or the conscious appreciation of conflict, and contrasts vividly in this regard with the previous record (Russell). She seems unaware of the psychosocial "price" of such things as marriage and motherhood. In a pitifully naive way she simply "wants" these events to "happen." Over five years of follow-up contact with Ellen have confirmed the characteristic of "wishful thinking" which is evident in this account. She has been rehospitalized several times and has made essentially no psychosocial progress.

5. Psychosis Associated with Psychedelic Drug Use in the Context of Adolescent Psychosexual Development

NANCY

In the following account we are presented with an example of an acute psychotic reaction associated with psychedelic drugs, used during a period of personal experimentation and attempted innovation. As Nancy describes it, "I had spent the whole summer testing out life styles." The conflict which was evoked by this testing led to an acute psychotic reaction in which guilt was apparently the initial driving emotion. The drug-precipitated psychotic reaction is an extremely important phenomenon for the understanding of psychotic states. It has long been recognized that certain pharmacologic substances, most notably cannabis, mescaline, amphetamine derivatives, lysergic acid diethylamine (LSD), and other indolalkylamines can produce an acute alteration of consciousness which bears a similarity to some forms of acute psychosis. In recent years clinicians have recognized another related phenomenon, namely instances in which the drug-induced alteration of consciousness persists and trails off into a psychotic state which is virtually indistinguishable from a psychotic reaction unrelated to drug use. We call this phenomenon a drug-precipitated psychosis. As yet we are unable to specify the unique constellation of ingredients that lead to such an outcome. Experience suggests, however, that certain individuals, by taking one of these drugs at particular times of developmental crisis, may evoke such a flood of unmanageable personal concerns that defensive structures are seriously breached for an extended period of time.

Nancy was a 20-year-old student in her second year at college. She was basically rather easy-going, but was particularly impressed by her father whom she described as a "man of principle." She felt implicitly his continual striving for achievement, as typified by his being awarded a Ph.D. just prior to her trip "out west to see what I could learn from others." There followed a series of attempts to live in the midst of a musical group she had met, but the behavior required of her in that context, primarily with regard to sexual experimentation and drug use, evoked an unmanageable degree of guilt and self-doubt. The psychosis which resulted was later described by Nancy during her recovery in the following terse phrases:

> I had spent the whole summer testing out life styles. I got involved with the student strike and was going to do street theater. There seemed to be too much polarization and I just wanted to talk to people. So I decided to take a trip out west to see what I could learn from others. I left after my father's graduation; he finally got his Ph.D. in June. I have always respected him for his intellect. When I got back from the trip I decided to go to Carolina to visit some kids who had a band there. That's when I

met this fellow Ray. I was fascinated by the life they lived—lots of drugs and sex. I felt this was the opening up of sex for me. However, this Ray turned out to be a real bum and sexually deviant. Still until I went to Carolina I had not had a boyfriend for three years. It was very intense. He told me he only had three jars of peanut butter and 66 capsules of mescaline. You have to understand that this was a complete change in life style for me, a new world completely. Some parts were beautiful. I felt I had to give up everything for sex. It was the only thing I could offer and I felt trapped. I took several capsules of mescaline over the two week period and began to see significance in things. They mentioned a dog and I thought I had become a dog sexually. Maybe, I thought, they were trying to teach me not to be up tight about sex. I began to have the notion that I would have a sex change operation. Maybe I was a guy trapped in a woman's body. My mind was running like crazy. Finally a friend agreed to drive me back home and during the trip things got much worse. Everything meant something more than it really was. I had the idea that I was supposed to approach my friend sexually. I felt I was trying very hard to understand the time in Carolina. When I finally got home my parents took me to a psychiatrist. I had a terrible fear of him. The whole waiting room of his office seemed to be filled with "props" to test me. I thought I was adopted, maybe sterile or suffering from mental retardation. I thought that the doctor would find something wrong with my body. A lady in the waiting room was giggling, and I thought that was a homosexual attempt. I saw a double rainbow and that made me believe there was hope. Noises were especially loud. My parents said I never slept. Anything I had ever had as a problem my mind dug up. Particularly problems with my father and with church. I thought I was going to have to choose between family and friends. I had written earlier to the minister asking that my church membership be dropped when I was 21 years old. My father really blew up after the minister told him. When I was sick at home, then, I had this idea that I had to marry my father in the Episcopal church. I thought the clock in the room was a camera and was taking pictures of my father and me as we sat on the sofa. I thought that I would be shot but would be born again. All the books I had ever read in my life seemed to come back to me. We went to see the family doctor who said I had just freaked out on drugs, but I had the idea something was seriously wrong with me. I thought I might have a terminal disease, be sterile or pregnant. When I told my mother I believed in God, I meant that I could take the bad news. So much was hitting my head at once. Every book I had read, every movie I had seen got involved. I remembered *Rosemary's Baby* and thought my father was the devil and would have intercourse with me. I thought an atomic bomb had been dropped and that there were people scratching on the window asking to be helped. This was one of the most vivid ideas I had. After my parents sat with me for nearly 3 days straight, they dressed me. I was seeing yellow halos around their heads. I thought I could tell my friends from my enemies by noticing whose arm was hot and whose was cold. I thought the police might want information about my friends and drugs from me. I often had a very strong urge to laugh. My body was supersensitive. I thought my bed would separate and that I would be

torn in half, that the top half of me belonged to the
devil and I would pay for what I had done. I believed I had to eat my sister and put her in my
stomach. I had read these creation myths in the past
so I had these bits of knowledge. They seemed to
return distorted and related to myself. I thought of
another fellow I knew named Buck, thought his
name meant "kick," that I had a drug habit. In bed
an image of a movie I'd once seen came to me—a
coke bottle tapping out a teletype message which
signified the end of the world. I thought my head
must be attached to a computer. I thought my brain
was being damaged and that I could feel cracks in it.
On my way to a hospital I noticed that everything
behind me was being burned or destroyed. Again
the idea of the atom bomb having been dropped
came to me. I thought I would die and be reborn. In
the hospital I thought one of the nurses was the
devil. That meant I was split in quarters—half of
me was a devil and half a woman. I could snap my
finger and hear a lady repeat "It's all right, dear, we
are all here to help you." A black technician drew
my blood, then stood in the window and spread her
arms. I thought she had crucified herself, and I
began to think about the political things I had been
involved with such as getting more black children
into school during the student strike. When I returned home I thought my parents wanted to hear
about my sex life. I must have felt very guilty, for it
upset my father greatly when I told him. At home I
"felt" noises in my body. A loud sound would register inside of me like a short shock. Also I was
afraid to move for fear that something terrible
would happen. I thought there was something registering my movements. I had an idea that I had to

save the neighborhood. Sometimes I felt only capable of destruction, other times I thought I could
save.

Comment

The onset of psychosis in this record is also set within
a context of adolescent psychosexual development.
Nancy had been a fairly representative college student in
many respects, although she harbored strong desires for
new and more independent experiences. She herself took
a great deal of initiative to seek out these experiences and
plunged into the task of "testing out life styles" with a
certain naiveté and recklessness. Although apparently
particularly uninformed and unprepared in the area of
sexual development, she hoped that her searchings
would lead to "the opening up of sex for me." She did
not anticipate the degree of exploitation to which she
would expose herself nor the severity with which her
own conscience would react to this experience. The account does not tell us why the issue of sexual guilt was so
unbearable for this young woman nor the precise role
the use of psychedelic drugs may have played in pushing
this conflict to unmanageable extremes at this precise
moment of her life. We have noted that conflicts which
are depicted in the phenomenology of psychotomimetic
drug-induced states can be understood as genuine conflictual issues for the individual which were under some
control prior to the drug-induced state. The drug experience appears to breach an intrapsychic buffer zone between certain kinds of current experience and internal
"symbols" of vulnerability.

This record demonstrates a number of state-determined (formal) characteristics of psychotic experience

which have been illustrated by previous accounts. The internal and external sensory overload is particularly apparent. "Noises were especially loud . . . . My body was supersensitive. . . . My mind was running like crazy. . . . Anything I had ever had as a problem my mind dug up. . . . All the books I had ever read in my life seemed to come back to me. . . . So much was hitting my head at once. . . . Every book I had read, every movie I had seen got involved. . . . I thought my head must be attached to a computer." Along with this perceptual and ideational overload there exists the experience that the personal relevance of the new sensory data is unequivocal. "I took several capsules of mescaline over the two week period and began to see significance in things. . . . Everything meant something more than it really was. . . . I had read these creation myths in the past so I had these bits of knowledge. They seemed to return distorted and related to myself." Thus far our illustration of this phenomenon of enhanced relevance has not provided any suggestion as to possible mechanisms involved in the production of this remarkable experiential state. We have simply observed that at times of intense anxiety and expectancy, the perceptual field is scrutinized for possible meaning or explanation and that psychological conflict becomes externalized or "projected." This is basically an irreducible observation. It is not at all clear how the mind is able to handle internal conflict in this fashion. Nor do we find this mechanism operative only in psychopathological states. This account illustrates other complex examples of externalization of conflict. "I could snap my finger and hear a lady repeat 'It's all right, dear, we are all here to help you'. . . . At home I 'felt' noises in my body. . . . A loud sound would register inside of me like a short shock." Thus the idea of reference may include experiences in which thoughts or actions actually seem to alter the external world; conversely, external perceptions may be felt to "register" internally. Such percepts must certainly serve to confirm the experience of enhanced relevance by creating a novel contiguity between fantasy and events which runs both ways. Further such a phenomenon is probably the basic experiential mechanism behind the ideation which is frequently found associated with "catatonic" states, namely that by movements or ideas an individual may feel he can exert extremely potent effects in the external world. Such experiences are suggested in the present account. "Also I was afraid to move for fear that something terrible would happen. I thought there was something registering my movements. I had an idea that I could save the neighborhood. Sometimes I felt only capable of destruction, other times I thought I could save." Thus the formal, state-determined aspects of this patient's experience are characterized by external and internal ideational overload which is felt as having direct relevance for the individual through experiential sequences in which the boundaries between fantasy and external perception are progressively broken down. The characteristics of the psychotic altered state in this instance are strikingly similar to other accounts presented in this volume. In the present case, however, the form of psychotic consciousness seems to have been triggered by psychedelic drug use. Certain drugs are thus apparently capable of setting into motion an internal experiential milieu characterized by a heightening of latent, individual-specific conflict. Drug use in this instance, therefore, probably contributed both to the timing and the form of the psychotic episode.

What then are the individual-determined aspects of the content of this experience? A variety of repressed personal memories have been activated by this episode. The phenomenon of hypermnesis, a formal aspect of psychotic experience, permits a memory flood to occur. The content of books and movies is recalled, as are religious concerns and intrafamilial conflicts. Equally personalized is the latent intrapsychic conflict depicted in the account, a theme which organizes the experiential data as the latent dynamic theme organizes the manifest data of the dream. With regard to the present account we can say that the organizing theme has to do primarily with dread. In other accounts we have seen predominant themes of wish-fulfillment, and such themes are present in rudimentary fashion in this record. ("I saw a double rainbow and that made me believe there was hope.") However, the primary theme is one of dreadful expectancy. "I thought I was adopted, maybe sterile or suffering from mental retardation. I thought that the doctor would find something wrong with my body. . . . I thought that I would be shot but would be born again . . . . I thought I might have a terminal disease, be sterile or pregnant. When I told my mother I believe in God I meant that I could take the bad news. . . . I thought my bed would separate and that I would be torn in half, that the top half of me belonged to the devil and I would pay for what I had done. . . . etc." Thus it seems plausible that punishment for sexual guilt is the underlying personal theme which the experiential data are called upon to confirm.

JACK

Jack, the author of this account, was a young man away from home for the first time during his freshman year in college. He had been raised in a family of several sons and no daughters, and his mother was a morally strict, devout woman whose rigidity Jack had internalized almost without modification. His father was an extremely successful businessman who was rarely home and who had participated to a very limited degree in the rearing of his sons. Jack chose a liberal college environment where young people experimented freely with sex and drugs. He felt pushed to "make it" in this environment, but found his own moral code in serious conflict with the morals of his peers. In this context he took LSD twice. During the drug experience he felt sufficient confidence to approach women for intimate relationships, but in reality this "confidence" was utilized merely in fanciful reveries which led him to "send vibrations" to certain women. In this context he developed an acute psychosis during which he wrote the following account:

> I feel that I have two worlds to live in. One is the "straight world" and the other is the "stoned world" (that stands for freedom and other high ideals that we value).
>
> I realize that the entire world has copped out and that people search for the romantic, but *really* don't want to find it. Like me; I never read through my diary, I always *think* about what is written. At times I am a genius, but at times I seem to be supporting things, arguing for things that people don't want to admit, because I can't admit them myself. I cannot go over and read my diary. I live in a drug related world. Drugs are *evil,* they make you feel great, but the *straight* world appears the same (drugged or undrugged). People do need narcotics and things to keep them going. Just as alcohol is bad, so is dope —they make you shun reality—but people don't want to admit it. How many times have I had to

admit this over the last weekend. (Read your diary and make sure to write it down while it is still fresh maybe real in your mind). I seem to be making a cop-out and succeeding at it and maybe the world wants me to do that. When I go "crazy" (when I'm straight) I dream weird dreams about romantic young boys being rejected by a girl, instead of fabricating something about a man who has eternal love and would sacrifice the world for his girl. I don't know whether I create my dream world or puncture other peoples'. I find that life is not romantic like everybody would wish it to be. But I find that people can't accept *me* having a romantic life, seeking romantic goals (truth). I find that this is why only certain people pick up hitchhikers. These "innocent ones" who are unafraid of hitchhikers either robbing or raping them . . . I wish I could complete this thought but I think I have an insight. . .

People are not viewing "reality" when they say I can't be having such a romantic affair. It seems strange, but you *lose* with Christ and you suffer so much more when you do good (absolute good) than when you're copping out, but holding Christ up as someone you admire and pretend you would like to be like (when you really don't want to be a martyr-type person). Maybe my 180° life is due to the schizophrenic structure of the world (are they wrong? or am I?).

The devil gets you and the only way towards the truth is to shun drugs, shun alcohol, shun selfishness (shun all the things worth living for in life). But that is a permanent—a long range goal. It seems that people only want short range goals— they will NEVER sacrifice *their* short range goals for long range goals unless they can get a guarantee

of some more short range goals. (If they think of it).
It seems to me that I succeed most when I compro-
mise myself most. It seems to me that love (Sandy's
love) has shown me the truth. I didn't need dope or
any escape from reality when I had Sandy. I feel that
true love—paradise— is so valuable, but you suffer
so much for it that people don't want it—they want
an easy way out—drugs, "fake" sex. It seems that
people will have no problems when they find love.
First love in woman and then a love of mankind
will be generated. It seems to me that drugs can be
dangerous because they attract you to the easy—to
the way of life that is a cop out, but that society
accepts and rewards—even when they "hold out"
for the idealistic goal—that is why idealism is a
dirty word to Americans. They favor cynicism
which is just another form of lying.

Americans have a tendency to discredit expression of feeling in terms of say, music, where there is
always a cry against "artificial devices—for artificial
devices sake." People don't believe that we can
adopt extensions of man (artificial device) to our
benefit. I would like to be an actor because to do so I
could live a life that I wanted to live. I would become the person I was supposed to be acting. I don't
think I could give out enough feeling and show of
emotion unless I really believed in the part that I
was playing. I could do a love scene so well except
that I would really have to have the girl that I was
supposed to be in love with. Only then could I give
100% of my emotion, only then could I overcome
the need for self-confidence so that I wouldn't be
afraid of having people laugh at me. I just couldn't
act "love" to another person because I would be too
hurt. Obviously I couldn't be a "great" actor but I

could at least have great performances. Act in something like Romeo and Juliet or West Side Story or Love Story. It seems to me now that I have to battle with the devil as all men have had to do. I feel stoned now and don't really want to write this down. My mind seems to want to forget, to shun reality. Time passed quickly when I was "straight." It passes so slowly now that I am stoned. Jack Johnson (desperate) 12:45 P.M. In-sights, heroes are what "real" people can't let themselves be. You are a hero when you don't have to cop out. When you seek the truth, find it, then tell everyone what the answer is. I have a weird idea about what craziness is right now. I will let her give in before I give in. I will cop out and let her call me before I call her. Why do people not know so much about Jesus' life when he was in his youth? Probably because he led a really swinging (evil) life but was able to transcend it and become the Son of God.

How come when I'm crazy people look up to me, or is it that I look down on them. I believe that searching for the truth is what everybody wants to do and what everybody claims to do. But for those heroes that search for it and find it society never *really* listens to them. They never act on it. My beard seems to have less growth after these three days. Perhaps I transcended that physical feature just as I transcended hunger and money and lots of other institutions that shackle me right now. Property and the search for fame make true love impossible although they certainly make cop-out love more valuable and more acceptable. I have genuine envy and therefore despise normal people while normal people at the same time envy and also therefore despise genius. I can control people but can either do

it for good, for "God" and be unselfish or I can do it
for the devil by being false to myself, by copping
out. It's too easy to do the latter. The "seduction"
will make me sell my soul to the devil. Genius is
insanity. To be a genius people have to *not* believe
you. You can't tell them great ideas, they will pros-
titute them, will not accept the truths. People believe what they want to believe. That is why they at
times disdain "dreamers" because dreamers seem to
have the answers to problems but people won't listen to them. I know that dope is ultimately harmful
but I can't convince any "non-straight" person of
that. I believe that I would not succumb to *any*
amount of popular pressure (psychological acceptance) even if the whole world were against me. All
I would need is one girl to love and understand me
and I would not need anything else. I need catharses
to make me great. I feel stoned but think that people
really do have an envious feeling about insane people because we have found happiness that we can
get just by making a choice, just by giving us a
choice in life between the straight world and the
stoned world. I am addicted to marihuana in a sense
because my mind will go crazy if I don't get high. I
feel that I am either a neurotic or a psychotic who is
not losing his head because he smokes dope and
falls in love and gets stoned in many ways. I think
that true genius-type people get their genius from
the crazy states and utilize it to write great poems
and make great works of art—for a certain woman
or for certain gods (money, fame). I feel like I could
be a great author by publishing "Books of the Obvious." People will buy them because they want to
see the obvious, the dull, the ridiculous (Nostalgia).
They want to do it because reality for them (like the

U.S.—Indochina War) is causing people to go back to nostalgia. It is so fearful they don't want to bear reality. They NEED TO ESCAPE. Dope and women are two things that can help you escape. I feel that my mind can rationalize (really solve problems). I have rationalized myself out of feeling the pain that I felt with Sandy. I have rationalized my way out of the greatest problem for me—love—and have therefore solved it. Look what I can do with problems (race, sex) that are less important to me than love. I bear the pain but get rewarded. I do things that people tell me not to do and then later on they eventually realize that I did the right thing. They say that I am wrong but later tell me that I am right after I have succeeded in my insane way.

Comment

This young man had found the first year at college an extremely trying experience. He was depressed almost from the very first and really did not understand the reasons why. During subsequent psychotherapy several factors became apparent. First of all, his parents were extremely ambitious for him and had managed to get him into a college which was very demanding academically. Whereas in high school he successfully obtained high marks with little effort, in the college setting a rather exacting self-discipline with regard to study habits was required. Jack was not used to tolerating frustration and depression. He often alluded to the fact that his wishes and desires—however extravagant—were always rapidly gratified by his mother. He later came to see this behavior on her part as a kind of bribe whereby she would tie him to herself emotionally, a need which seemed to arise out of loneliness and frustration in her marriage. In addition, she imbued him with her own uncompromising rigidity regarding sexual matters. Jack thus approached the challenges of the college experience with serious built-in constraints to his own development. He had little tolerance for loneliness, frustration, or realistic problem solving, and he felt uniquely bound to his mother's morality, sensing that to explore his own developing sexual life was in some way to defile her. During the acute psychosis he expressed the conviction that if he were to find a girlfriend, his mother would probably die.

Thus, throughout his entire first semester he managed to dodge the pain occasioned by separation from home and confrontation with new challenges by smoking a great deal of marijuana. He fantasized a great deal about a close, intense love relationship which would also, in the pattern of the relationship with his mother, protect him from the demands of actually forming peer relationships. In this context he took LSD twice, an interval of about one week separating the two experiences. It was, therefore, the interaction of this individual psychosocial history, the growth tasks presented by the college milieu, and the psychotomimetic drug experience which determined the timing of the psychotic episode.

The formal (state-determined) aspects of this psychotic episode shared many of the qualities of the records previously presented, although they are not all specifically described in Jack's writing. However, since I worked with this patient during his acute hospitalization and for over a year as an outpatient, I had numerous opportunities to hear the details of his acute psychosis. He apparently initially experienced a number of "connections" between his own thoughts and events in the external world. He would "think something" and have the experience that reality would conform to his thought. For instance, on one occasion he "thought" that a door should open and it did. Such experiences confirmed in his own mind a potent relationship between fantasy and changes in reality and led him to entertain the notion that he had supernatural powers. He said at one point, "Reality will just have to conform to my way of thinking." These ideas of unique relatedness between his thoughts and external reality expanded to take in worldwide events. Soon after hospitalization he wrote, "I feel that there is a relationship between the news and what actually happens to me. It seems that when I am blue, so is the world. Yesterday the U.S. was losing in Indochina, whereas today it seems to be doing O.K." We noted similar experiential characteristics in the account immediately preceding this one (Nancy). Jack's writing is fragmented and difficult to follow, suggesting a constant intrusion of ambivalent and competing thoughts. He later wrote, "I believe that I had the key to the door of perception but misused it in some way. My ego was more like a selective sieve rather than a control mechanism." Thus, the form of his psychotic experience occasioned by psychedelic drug use appears to have led to ideational overload, an enhanced sense of the material efficacy of mere thought with attendant grandiose ideas, and to a breakdown in intrapsychic defenses which had previously tenuously contained certain individual-specific conflicts.

These conflicts seem to have centered around the need for a safe, childlike, and guileless bond with a mothering figure as opposed to the demands and risks of age-appropriate psychosexual development.

When I go "crazy" (when I'm straight) I dream
weird dreams about romantic young boys

being rejected by a girl, instead of fabricating something about a man who has eternal love and would sacrifice the world for his girl . . . It seems that people will have no problems when they find love. First love in woman and then a love of mankind will be generated . . . all I would need is one girl to love and understand me and I would not need anything else . . . Why do people not know much about Jesus' life when he was in his youth? Probably because he led a really swinging (evil) life but was able to transcend it and become the Son of God.

Personalized aspects of the content of his psychotic experience include not only manifestations of the specific conflictual issues but also evidence of characteristic defenses. In Jack's case, avoidance of pain by wish-fulfilling, fantasied mastery of problems was a characteristic approach to developmental challenges which was intensified by a drug-induced psychotic consciousness.

I seem to be making a cop-out and succeeding at it and maybe the world wants me to do that . . . I didn't need dope or any escape from reality when I had Sandy. I feel that true love—paradise—is so valuable, but you suffer so much for it that people don't want it—they want an easy way out—drugs, "fake" sex . . . My mind seems to want to forget, to shun reality . . . It is so fearful they don't want to bear reality. . . . They NEED TO ESCAPE. Dope and women are two things that can help you escape. I feel that my mind can rationalize (really solve problems). I have rationalized myself out of feeling the pain I felt with Sandy. I have

rationalized my way out of the greatest problem for me—love—and have therefore solved
it.

In the two records presented in this chapter, psychedelic drug use has occurred in a particular developmental context, a context in which psychotic disorders may
emerge without the use of drugs, as we have seen. The
psychotic experience which thus ensues is characterized
by an internal structure with regard to form and content
very much akin to that which we have encountered in
previous records. There thus appears to be a unique syn-
ergism between the disarticulation of consciousness produced by certain drugs and that which emerges in the
course of psychotic reactions not associated with drug
use.

6. *Psychosis Associated with Childbirth*

LORETTA

Thus far we have emphasized that the timing of acute psychotic episodes is usually associated with certain maturational challenges in late adolescence which lie at the very core of human psychological growth and individuation. We have noted that successful psychosexual development in late adolescence requires a capacity for bearing loneliness and loss, for the establishment of gratifying peer relationships, and for the reasonable modulation of guilt. The preceding accounts have described the turmoil which may ensue when individuals approach these challenges ill-equipped or ill-prepared in these areas. Other human experiences, including marriage and childbirth, which build upon the tasks of adolescence, put these and other capacities to test. This chapter and the one which follows are examples of psychotic reactions which occurred in the contexts of childbirth and marriage.

The young, unmarried woman who wrote this account became pregnant while attending college and decided to withdraw from school and return to live with her father and stepmother. Her own mother had died when Loretta was 14 following a long illness during which Loretta had witnessed several episodes of severe bleeding. Although she received no support from the father of the child, she decided to carry the pregnancy to term. Prior to the delivery she worked in a convalescent home and spent, in her own words, "long hours watching people die, cleaning up blood—exhausting work." At the end of each day she would return home and retire to her room to read books on psychology. During this period there were many exchanges between Loretta and her father, who was extremely angry about the pregnancy. The father would become periodically enraged, call Loretta a whore and insist that he was not going to kill himself worrying about her. Such an outburst occurred following delivery of the child when Loretta returned home. She then placed the child for adoption and sought psychiatric assistance which led to hospitalization for an acute psychotic episode. Following discharge she led a very unsettled life characterized by frequent moves and by brief affairs culminating in a second hospitalization approximately one year later. It was during this latter hospitalization that the following "letters" were written.

Dear David,

My doctor here is truly a wonderful man whom I love very much. I shall be able to rest and absorb a tremendous change, the metamorphosis which I am going through, such a tremendous and beautiful change. At the moment I must and am redirecting an enormous amount of frustration and anger. For the first time in my life I have felt uncontrollable rage at a mentally, emotionally, and physically unbearable situation and I emphasize this is the first time in my life that I am now one hundred percent, that I have ever felt this rage. So David when you asked me "Loretta how can you be so sweet?", here is your answer. Because I never had sufficient pressure placed on me to feel pure hatred and pure anger my reaction was always tempered. Your talk about guns and violence freaked me out but now, damn it, you are right. I am lucky in the sense that I am learning about violence, hatred and anger in a "safe environment" which is full of do-gooders and objective scientists, nurses aides, doctors, medical students and social workers. You once expressed an interest to know my soul, well you shall know it through my letters. My bond with you shall grow ever deeper—constructive destruction, revolution, evolution in the name of truth and peace and love. However, I am still grooving with the Bible, and with Christ, Buddha, Mahatma Ghandi. All along the way my femininity keeps knocking at the door saying, "I love you David." I did not know that bottomless love could grow but it has. The prehistoric monsters who dwell within the deepest darkest depths of the lakes of North America (I decided this was a good analogy for what you were stirring within me).

Dear David,

I am so love-starved it drives me crazy. I had a visitor the other night who gave me a beautiful picture of a fish. He feels that number eleven is the cosmic number. I also am seven and eleven. My love for you changes and grows. Each day I am filling in the details of my infinite love for you. I must be calm and serene, for this is a tremendous task. Please write me as often as you can. I feel quite happy during the day, yet I cannot help but feel desperately trapped. Everything and everyone is being distorted. Perfectly nice people I see as wardens and my behavior is becoming distorted and exaggerated so that I cannot think clearly.

What I am commencing to write is the culmination of two years of reflection upon experience, quite wide experience and reflection. I believe as does the British psychiatrist Laing that the patient's hopes and dreams do remain very much intact and unscarred by the outward signs of madness. I have reflected deeply on my condition and particularly during the years of emotional stress, during which I strove desperately to maintain an equilibrium so that I would be able to be a true mother to my child which at the time of her conception was a physical manifestation of my desire to find a childlike balance within myself. I was born in the hospital on January 20, 1948. I do not know the exact time though I wish to find out because I believe in the science of astrology. I have many early memories that I distinctively associate with the smell of vaseline during my babyhood. As well as my dislike for bland cream of wheat. I have memories of smells and sounds and many experiences during my first four years of life. This is an attempt to emerge from my own individual universal chaos, at the moment I am considering thinking about Milton's *Paradise Lost*, and the fact that I should find an appropriate—is Muse the word? I have much to say, my story will be long and I hope some day beneficial to others who attempt to emerge into the light from darkness. My favorite words are metamorphosis, kaleidoscope. I am relieved that at last I shall be capable of expressing all that I have bottled up or expressed in immature ineffective ways. I was going to say that I must structure this, however, this is not true I think a natural symmetry will reveal itself and actually the purpose of this journal would be somewhat defeated if I made a conscious effort to structure it. Rather I shall allow my thought to flow freely thus achieving a more thorough catharsis. Can I love? Yes, I remember the underlying scorn and rejection of myself, empty meaningless sex. Why do I indulge in your vacuum of pleasure? No pleasure for me. Do I fear the total release. Where are you orgasm, where are you release from thought, release from fear. Where are you free energy to direct into creative channels.

When I actually "blew up" I had delusions that my father was going to kill me and I pretended to have pains and they rushed me in an ambulance to the hospital. When I got ill I woke my father up at night in a controlled but desperate attempt to find help in my overwrought state. He got up and I started to read a letter to him, a letter I had written in an attempt to understand where my head was at and he got mad at me and walked over to the wall, screwed up his face and fist and nearly put his fist through the wall. He said "Jumping Jesus Christ, a police record! Me? For that slut, a police record. Jumping Jesus Christ." Then he took another drink and continued to holler and swear and drink. I was in the bathroom washing and he came up to me his face was bright red, his eyes were bulging. I had checked the rifle in his room to see if it was loaded before I went to the maternity home. I got dressed, wrapped up the baby and went to the neighbors who took me to the police station. My father came and got me and brought me home. He simply sat in his chair drinking and saying in a

louder and louder voice "My baby, My baby." I told
him that after all his parents had to get married. I
did not say it to be mean nor to throw it in his face,
but he said, "You bitch," and from that time on he
regressed and plunged further and further into his
drinking. He told me that he was not going to die
because of me, that if his blood pressure went up
higher he would kick me out because he wasn't
going to die because of me. In the convalescent
home I emptied catheters, I washed down and dis-
infected beds and bed stands; then I would go home
and read, often with every cell in my body screaming with the pain of exhaustion. I was pregnant and
desperately reading and thinking, preparing myself
to be a mother, a real mother. When I kept changing clothes and trading I was playing role after role
and trying to find the one that suited me. I used to
go around giving people things that they needed,
symbols of what they needed.

Dear Phillip,

I'm going to be firm with you in this letter because I care about your welfare, your mental and
emotional welfare. You must straighten out the
maze of emotions, loneliness, rejection, anger and
hatred that have formed a knot in you or you will
never be able to enter into a balanced relationship
with me or anyone. The circumstances that caused
this are beyond your control. The positive aspect is
that we are young and able to be healed before we
become more and more emotionally disturbed. I feel
that you are too intelligent, sensitive and talented to
waste any more time. I also believe in certain mystical phenomena which seem to me to be directly re-

lated to cosmic consciousness. However, before you (or myself) can put themselves wholeheartedly into psychic phenomena and the study of the Trinity and God (a la Jung—he is a good place to start) we must face and overcome the bottled-up pain of repressed, confused emotion. It hurts but like having a baby it is a wonderful creative pain, for one is reborn to live a balanced life. Your flight into "The realms" are often I think an evasion of the painful human emotions. I used to do the same thing. Philip, underneath your confusion lives an extraordinarily beautiful person, a person with a tremendous amount to offer the world. You must fight to fill that void. It pains me to see you wallowing in the mire of guilt and emotional pain and confusion. It rather excites me to see you struggle, however, because I am sure that eventually you will enter the light after having experienced a catharsis similar to my own.

[At this point a number of arithmetical calculations are made which link the birth dates of the patient to the birth dates of her mother and the child she bore. Also listed is the day her mother died.]

Hi, I have something extremely important to tell you about the number seven which to me means "child" (I am the Alpha and Omega C = 3, D = 4, totalled is 7. Your room at the hotel is 107 which equals seven. The address where I now am is 34 Oak Street 3 + 4 = 7). I always dwelled on the number even as a child, arranging titles and such things into groups of seven. I'll write more about this when I'm high and things are clicking. I need books on Astrology, Numerology, E.S.P., and so forth.

Dear David,

You are a breath of fresh air and I love you. Sevens! I was born in 1947 which adds up to twenty-one. My mother died when I was fourteen in 1961. 6 + 1 = 7. I had my child on December 21, 1968 (eight and six is fourteen). She weighed six pounds eight ounces (eight and six is fourteen). She was born at 12:52 P. M. (seven minutes before one. This is the dawning of the age of Aquarius (selfless love + 1969). Obviously I am a seven child. 3 = Trinity, 4 = Man. Ten is the cosmic number. Note the shape of 10 and 11-two complete people, two whole people —hermaphrodites. Cool down! I have to do the same myself and here's what I believe: you and I have a mission on earth, we know, we are enlightened. And our mission is to set people free. We may be reincarnations of "people" who have achieved nirvana (freedom) and who have chosen to return to earth to help set people free. I am speaking to you and I am the Sunshine, the Light and the Way. I was named in my father's dream and my name means the light. Stick to earthly drugs, not LSD or mescaline. Read about the Hindu Religion and Buddha. Christ is the fish symbolically. We are both sevens and elevens, total people and we shall be together soon. Let's find a place where life is not a hassle, where we can talk a lot and delve into books and learn from others and find our psychic cosmic family and try to figure ourselves out further. Drugs if necessary, but I believe that we can do this naturally. I send you the Rainbow and the Sun, Love and Kisses and Smiles and Lollipops and a little bit of heaven. We must talk about the games we played as children, numbers, colors and so forth. I patterned everything into sevens. Read Carl G. Jung.

Dear David,

I am fuming and my anger grows as I remain in this insane place full of insane doctors, insane nurses, and insane aides. These past few days have been hell. I fought for years to free myself from my family situation only to be thrown into a locked ward of a state nuthouse. It is terribly frustrating to be constantly misinterpreted. I never had a mental breakdown, I generated a "natural trip" last year and my head was together. I try to explain that I have a natural joy inside. When I have a balanced "high" I feel like a figure in white walking on a path of fantastically colored flowers. It's so hard for me to contain my rage. I am a tempest also, David, a raging tempest. I can tell you about reality, about the patients in the convalescent homes who were not allowed to die in dignity, about blood gushing from her mouth as she died and convulsed and was still and cold and gray, about cleaning up the dark red clotted blood all over the sink, blood which my mother had vomited, about washing dead bodies and so forth. So Little Miss Sunshine is not a hot house plant in an unreal world. I know, yet I also have a tremendous faith in God and in myself and in the Way, the Light and the Truth. The truth shall set you free. Fight for Christ's truth, fight for Love and World Peace. I love you, David, I love you with my musical kaleidoscopic metamorphosing soul. David, my before, during, and after the storm, the tempest, the depths of which stir my eternal serene joy.

Comment

This account is remarkable for the affective force which is conveyed in the psychotic experience. Alternatively intense anger and euphoric interludes characterize the experiential state. The heightened sense of the significance of ideation and the playful use of this experience is noteworthy. The drive to significance, connectedness, and meaning is illustrated by the use of the numbers. Hence the altered state is characterized by affective intensity, a sense of purposive mission, a conviction of heightened relevance of percept for thought and vice versa. All of these qualities can be seen as giving an altered form to her experience. This form determines that her experience will be intense, personally convincing, seductive, and to some degree indelible.

The altered form of consciousness does not determine the *content* of her experience, although it permits emergence of certain personally-relevant dynamic themes and emotions. For instance, by the rather arbitrary use of near-coincidences with numbers, she connects herself, her boyfriend, her dead mother, and her child—individuals with focal significance for her own particular life. The manner in which the psychotic altered state evokes a particular theme and binds the present to the past is illustrated by the following section of the account:

> I am a tempest also, David, a raging tempest. I
> can tell you about reality, about the patients in
> the convalescent homes who were not allowed
> to die in dignity, about blood gushing from
> her mouth as she died and convulsed and was
> still and cold and gray, about cleaning up the
> dark red clotted blood all over the sink, blood
> which my mother had vomited. . . .

The indefiniteness in the account of the "her" from whose mouth blood once gushed joins the more recent traumatic experiences in the convalescent home to the earlier ones related to her mother's illness. Another content manifestation of personal significance in this account is the rage expressed, which undoubtedly has its origins in the sequence of traumatic abandonments which Loretta had suffered. A mother who died tragically, an unfeeling, alcoholic father, and a rejecting lover—all have contributed to the justifiable, pent-up fury which bursts forth in the acute psychosis.

Yet another personalized content theme in this account are the expressions of efforts toward role definition. "I was pregnant and desperately reading and thinking, preparing myself to be a mother, a real mother. When I kept changing clothes and trading, I was playing role after role and trying to find the one that suited me."

From one point of view there is an overall illusory aspect to the account. Life conflicts are portrayed as having been understood and to some degree mastered. Thus, while there is hope there is obviously no real awareness of the journey ahead, no appreciation for the work and time that will be required to come to terms with the anger, the sense of loss and abandonment and the fear that were engendered in her experiences with her parents and by the birth and loss of her child. Thus the altered experiential state both clarifies, promotes, and distorts. It lays bare some of the essential conflictual areas and creates a kind of premature sense of mastery which may inspire hopefulness. It is prophetic yet incomplete. It deludes and oversimplifies. Treatment cannot continue so long as these distortions prevail. Yet the wise therapist will not be completely put off by the illusory mastery of conflict in some psychotic states. If he can learn it for himself, he may be able to help his patient distinguish authentic hope from wishful thinking.

7. Psychosis Associated with Marital Crisis

ELIZABETH

This account was written at my request by a 32-year-old married woman, one week following a six-week hospital stay. She apparently agreed to write the account to "have the whole experience behind me," and in that frame of mind she presented it to me. The immediate events leading up to hospitalization are alluded to in the document. Elizabeth was a very sensitive, though non-assertive, woman who was experiencing increasing conflict in her marriage of eight years. Her own father was an extremely critical and demeaning man whose influence Elizabeth had hoped to escape by her marriage. Her husband, she increasingly perceived, was not the capable, protecting man she had hoped but was quite insecure and in need of support himself. His responses to her inadequacies were frequently thoughtless and abusive. He suggested, for instance, that she "go have some affairs" so that she could be a more satisfying sexual partner for him. She was, however, bound to the relationship by the same lack of confidence which made her relatively ineffective in it. In the context of this conflict she became psychotic, and she wrote the following document as a description of the onset of that experience:

It began at the first session of Mrs. Morris' class on the disciplining of children. My husband and I went together, and there were four other couples.

Earlier in the fall I had told Mrs. Morris about my marital problems and how worried I was because of what it might be doing to my children. As she talked, I began to think she had consulted other people about my husband and myself, even my parents and neighbors, and was using facts from my life to illustrate discipline situations. I was very happy that she had decided to help me, as it seemed to me. From things Mrs. Morris said, I believed she had consulted Dr. Wilson, the pediatrician. I thought of Dr. Wilson as the kind of man I would liked to have had as a father. I thought that he would be present at a social gathering scheduled for the Sunday after Valentine's Day, though I had no real reason to suspect this. Mrs. Morris commented how important to a child's security and peace of mind was the care for his physical needs. I thought I had paid too much attention to my children's emotional needs forgetting the importance of their physical welfare. I thought Sandra might have a heart condition because I had pushed her too much. I thought both of the children might become deaf due to my failure to take them to the doctor in time. I felt guilty about smoking when I was pregnant with Ellen and when I nursed her. I thought that smoking was injuring my own health; sometimes I tried to stop, other times I wished I were dead, and smoked even the dirty cigarette butts lying around.

I believed that I was an "emotionally disturbed" person; I believed my husband was something or other, but I didn't know what except that it scared me to think he might break down and "do something." As she talked, Mrs. Morris' eyes had a twinkle. Later, when I began to think I had been hypnotized, I thought it had started that evening.

Thursday through Tuesday

Thoughts spun around in my head and everything, objects, sounds, events, etc., took on special meanings for me. Childhood feelings began to come back, as symbols and bits from past conversations went through my head: I felt like I was putting the pieces of a puzzle together. I thought understanding myself better would help me with conflicts that I felt compelled to resolve; I wanted to grow up and feel the way a 33-year old woman was supposed to. I had the feeling of losing everything. I related this feeling with what Mrs. Morris had said about toilet training. I remembered as a child I had been constipated, and recalled vividly one time when I was given an enema. I related this sensation of losing everything with going to the bathroom. I couldn't find anything, like shoes, socks, etc. This problem got more acute as the week went along. I shed clothing, and tried to wear the appropriate clothing befitting my age and my role. I thought I had to wear the appropriate costume in order to behave appropriately.

Mrs. Morris had remarked how easily a child can adopt a role in play: just a hat is enough to make a child feel that part. She also mentioned how children love to wear sneakers. I thought she was talking about my own childhood situation when she told us the story of a very creative child who had charmed her parents out of her share of attention—that I was so "creative" that I could play any role almost to the point of convincing myself of the reality of the play, that it had gotten to the point that I could imagine everyone's point of view and had no identity for myself; that I could slip into a role without even knowing about it. I felt sometimes when I was in the house that I was hiding, like a cowboy expecting an ambush. I felt that adults had to be properly dressed else they would mix roles and get all mixed up about what they were. I thought that crazy people when they mixed costumes were dangerous. So, dressed in my winter coat (which made me feel mannish) and snowboots (cowboy-style) I did some research in my head and discovered what an "irrestible impulse" was. And I, mentally spinning, dangerously dressed, saw a cap pistol on the ground and felt like picking it up and shooting it. Then I thought how many crazy people there might be who would have this same feeling and not be able to control it.

After that, I felt it a dire emergency to run to the store and buy boots and shoes appropriate to my role as housewife and mother. I shed my winter coat and substituted an old mouton Smith College coat, I threw away my black stockings, because they were old lady's stockings. I noticed sometimes I even walked like an old lady. My father had explained to me how my grandmother had died when he visited at Christmastime. Although I could remember nothing about her, I thought I had mimicked her and played grandmother as a child.

Mrs. Morris mentioned how disturbing it was to a child to have toys taken away or thrown away before the child was old enough to understand the reason for it. I felt she was referring to my family's move from Connecticut to New York when I was four and a half. A lot of my toys I never saw again. I

thought this was why it was so painful for me in my
marriage which had prided itself for a long time on
the lack of material possessions. I thought my reason for feeling Connecticut was home was that I
was unconsciously trying to recover my possessions.
I began to think Dr. Wilson had been my pediatrician when I was four and we lived in Hartford; that
Mrs. Morris was the nursery school teacher for my
brother's nursery school. I began to think I was
hypnotized so that I would remember what had
happened in the first four and a half years of my life.
I thought that my parents had supplied information about the nursery school teacher and pediatrician to someone—perhaps my husband—with the
hope that I would be able to straighten myself out
by remembering the early years. I thought that my
husband and I in our marital relationship had become homosexuals, and the thought terrified me. I
felt that I couldn't do two things at once, that taking care of two children was perhaps impossible for
me. I felt as if I were love and hate with nothing in
the middle, that everything was opposites; but that I
was fighting myself so that the little girl of four and
a half would grow up quickly, and so that I could
be a woman and a good mother to my children.

As this feeling became more desperate I made
myself go through certain "rituals": such as the dis-
carding of clothing (I even threw away my husband's western boots, meaning to tell him we'd better stop playing cowboy). I felt as if I might be becoming dangerous to my children. So a voice in my
head kept saying, "You must protect the children."
I put all "phallic symbols," knives, knitting needles, etc., in a suitcase. I put the suitcase in the garbage. I began to lose more control over myself,

which worried me. I made the gesture of throwing a stone through the window, but caught myself before I actually did it. I felt more and more as if I had been hypnotized, that there were microphones hidden all over the house, that everybody was helping me and giving me a chance to go through this ordeal. I even thought at this time that my husband might be in on the plot to "save" me. My neighbor's oldest daughter seemed to drop over to see how I was; I thought all my neighbors had been told and knew what was going on, and were protecting me.

I remembered telling a friend that if everything could be turned inside out, that if everyone helped me and took my side, so that I wouldn't have any fear of being ostracized, then I could do anything I aspired to do. I also believed anyone could will themselves to be their own image of greatness. I thought this was what was happening. I thought something I heard on the radio was a message for me; that *Time Magazine* had an article written for me. Everything got increasingly symbolic. I began sleeping only two hours a night, seeing movies in my head till I fell asleep. For some reason I didn't feel exhausted during the day.

Cigarettes became phallic symbols. I kept lighting them and throwing them in the toilet. When I felt good I noticed I didn't smoke; I forgot them. The *Time Magazine* article was about present-day sex and morals. It said that a certain group was trying to discover the difference between good orgasm and bad orgasm, that one made a person feel good, and the other made a person feel bad. "Aha!" I said to myself. "Could it be that . . .?" Since our marriage seemed to sink or swim on the basis of our sexual relations, the article was very pertinent. Often I had felt "bad" after ours. My oldest daughter made some valentines with my help. We cut out hearts. Later, the hearts became bloody hearts in my mind, as well as love ones. Now that it was almost Wednesday again, I remembered Mrs. Morris had said we should attend her discipline class "religiously" or not attend at all. The word "religiously" and other words from other past conversations during the fall and summer months came back to me during this week, and seemed to take on new significance. I increasingly began to feel I was experiencing something like mystical revelations. I thought about the Sunday social gathering at which I thought Dr. Wilson would be, and it became a kind of destination. If I could last till then, I would be absolved of the sins I felt I was guilty of, and that I would be readmitted to the land of decent people.

Wednesday

We took a walk, my children, the dog, and I. I began to worry about my ability to take care of my children; but the voice kept saying, "You must protect the children." So I willed myself to be very, very careful. I held their hands firmly while walking along the road. But a car stopped as we were waiting to cross the road; the woman said to me, "So that's the dog that almost killed my dog. I see you have him on the leash now." I thought, "Oh, fooey!" and my left hand let go of Ellen just as a car coming the other way tried to squeeze between us and the car that had stopped. Instead, I said, "Yes, you don't have to worry; we walk him now." I was alarmed that I had let go of Ellen, and thought I was being tested as to whether I was a good mother or not, and that this would be a strike against me. I thought the left hand was the bad hand, the hand of hate. I had the illusion of believing that hand had grown stronger. The proof being that when playing the piano the left hand was getting louder.

I had made another appointment with Mrs. Morris for 1:30 or so in the afternoon. I had planned to talk with her about what was going on. But I changed my mind and went instead to introduce her to Sandra whom she hadn't met, and to show her a good drawing I had made. I was very happy because I felt like myself. I felt I had to go through the day until the meeting at Mrs. Morris', and then I'd be able to function as a girl, as me, Elizabeth.

After leaving Mrs. Morris we drove around, my head getting more and more mixed up. I had told Sandra we would go to the Stamford Museum. As we went along the parkway, the sun shone on the windshield and blinded me so that I had to pull over to the side of the road to clean the windshield. I got out of the car and saw the cars coming at me very fast. I saw the real danger and felt it was like a new experience for me. I thought I was being shown the real things to fear in place of the old general panic and feeling of inadequacy. Now I would see a symbol and there would be a "boing" in my mind, and I'd remember something and its significance in my life. I drove the car as if I were a child driving for the first time. I got to the Stamford Museum about 5:00. We ran around looking at the animals. I had a thought of how it would be to be an elephant in a cage; and then I was distressed, and as we went out I yelled at the sky "I'm not an elephant. I'm Elizabeth." (When I gave birth to Ellen I described to my husband that I trumpeted like an elephant.) Then a man asked me about my dog. He said something about being connected with the Psychology Department. I wanted to ask him to help me because I realized I was in no condition to drive the car. But I couldn't ask. I thought this man was in on the plot. I felt "they" wanted me to behave in a certain way. Symbols and events seemed to clue me in on the way to behave. On the way to the store I had a flat tire. I thought this was planned also. At the gas station the men smiled at me with twinkles in their eyes, and I felt very good, and I saw smiling men's faces in the sky and the stars twinkling, and stars twinkling in their eyes. I felt better than I ever had in my life.

There was another voice now saying to me: "Go towards what makes you feel good." We drove to the supermarket. The car parked next to ours had an elderly man sitting in it. He looked like a priest dressed in red and white. "Boing," it reminded me of my grandmother's funeral. In the supermarket—boing—I looked in my messy purse, and thought how like an old lady's purse. I began to feel that we were all schizophrenics; me, my husband, Sandra, and Ellen, my mother and father. At the supermarket I got the makings for spaghetti. Later, eating it, it reminded me of blood and flesh—boing—and my husband who liked it was then under suspicion. I thought he might have murdered someone, and many more morbid thoughts of this kind. I began to be afraid I would get out of control and kill my children and myself or that my husband would. Returning to the house I could hardly do anything. I couldn't find things, I couldn't concentrate on anything I tried to do. I walked aimlessly around the house. Somehow I fed the children and dressed for the second meeting with Mrs. Morris. I tried to dress in clothes that I would have been comfortable in when I was in college.

The babysitter came and I drove to pick up my husband. All the good feeling left me when he got in the car. When we arrived at the meeting I could neither talk nor listen to what was said; I was as uncomfortable as I used to be. I felt Mrs. Morris was trying to draw me out, but I felt very uncomfortable.

Returning home, I felt very defeated and very desperate. I asked my husband to make love to me even though I had my period. He did. We were both disappointed. Later, I imagined he had used a knife. I felt like a whore. I smelled cigar smoke coming from downstairs. This was my husband's first cigar since we got married. I thought this unusual and began to get scared of him. I realized that he wasn't part of the plot. But I thought someone had given him the cigar as a kind of pacifier. I thought he might be cracking up. We stayed up all night long talking. I thought he might have done something really awful. I grew terrified of him. I thought he would kill me if he lost control of himself. I thought there were people watching the house, and that they would intervene if something awful happened. I began to tremble, shiver, my heart pounded. I paced back and forth. I thought that something my brother did when we were little scared me a great deal, but being loyal I couldn't tell on him. I thought I had the same relationship with my husband, that he was bad, and I couldn't tell on him. I was afraid my husband would never call the doctor even if I were dying. I suggested once that I was having a heart attack, and that maybe we should call the doctor. Finally, he did.

The doctor called back at a moment when I was most terrified about what my husband was saying; I thought people were listening to us talk, and the phone rang purposely to distract him from going on with what he was saying. I thought if I could just manage to survive until Sunday everything would be all right. I thought an experiment was being carried on, that I or anyone could will themselves not to die, to have or have not, a heart attack, etc. and that a test was being made. Valentine's Day I thought of as a pagan's Good Friday. In the hospital, I wasn't convinced that all of this was delusion until Sunday had passed. Also, I thought I had regressed so far and decivilized myself so much, that I was nothing more than a wild woman, an Indian.

Comment

The timing of this psychotic illness is related to Elizabeth's perception that her marriage is in serious difficulty. She has endured years of abuse and disrespect which she has been unable to question; moreover she blames herself for her husband's erratic, uncaring behavior. Intimidated throughout her early years by her own father, she has been unable to manage that degree of healthy self-assertion as an adult which would have been required for the maintenance of her marriage. Her guilt and lack of competence in her role as wife and mother paralyze her, as does her fear that her husband will abandon her. This impasse ushers in a psychotic illness.

This document is a particularly illustrative example of the interaction between form and content during an acute psychotic state. The aura of hopeful yet fearful expectancy pervades the account. All perceptual processes are at the command of and in the service of the desire to unravel, to understand, and finally to *know* and to know with security. This expectant air is coupled with a repetitive experience that real "connections" are being made. The account is filled with evidence of a kind of autosuggestibility—a state wherein the varied data of consciousness coalesce around some dynamic thread and, with critical judgment suspended, achieve the immediate status of significance and relevance. " 'Aha!' I said to myself. 'Could it be that?'. . . . Now I would see a symbol and there would be a 'boing' in my mind, and I'd remember something and its significance in my life." Here we find dissected the critical mental ingredients which lead to the "idea of reference"—severe anxiety, ideational overload, suspension of critical judgment, and the internally veridical "Aha" experience. The mental apparatus is thus geared to achieve meaning at any price.

Another aspect of the altered state in psychosis which is illustrated by this document is the hypermnesis with regard to the events of childhood.

> Childhood feelings began to come back as symbols and bits from past conversations went through my head . . . I began to think I was hypnotized so that I would remember what had happened in the first four and a half years of my life . . . I thought that my parents had supplied information about the nursery school teacher and pediatrician to someone—perhaps my husband—with the hope that I would be able to straighten myself out by remembering the early years.

This aspect of the psychotic state has not been sufficiently emphasized. As we have noted, the ideational flood in acute psychosis comes both from the external perceptual field and from the internal store of memories and feelings. Such internal stimuli are also grist for the delusional mill.

This account further illustrates the intrusion of ideation concerning growth strivings and identity formation which we have previously noted in other documents.

> I felt like I was putting the pieces of a puzzle together. I thought understanding myself better would help me with conflicts that I felt compelled to resolve; I wanted to grow up and feel the way a 33-year old woman was supposed to . . . I felt as if I were love and hate with nothing in the middle, that everything was opposites, but that I was fighting myself so that the little girl of four and a half would grow up quickly and so that I could be a woman and a good mother to my children.

Such expressions of conflict and desire for personal change are a common but not invariable aspect of conscious experience during certain psychotic states. We have previously suggested that this experience of conflict may have prognostic significance. At the very least its presence makes possible a more rapid achievement of a working consensus between patient and therapist.

The content of the psychotic ideation described by this individual centers around the recollection of myriad events and conflicts experienced during her own developmental years.

> I remembered as a child I had been constipated and recalled vividly one time when I was given an enema . . . I thought she was talking about my own childhood situation when she told us the story of a very creative child who had

charmed her parents out of her share of attention . . . I felt she was referring to my family's move from Connecticut to New York when I was four and a half.

Other examples are cited above in reference to the state-related phenomenon of hypermnesis. Furthermore, the latent theme of overwhelming fear or dread is determined by Elizabeth's own intrapsychic makeup. The fear—like a nightmarish dream—has two determinants in this instance. One is the internal guilt related to her own excessively harsh judgment of herself as wife and mother. The second is her fantasied helplessness in the face of anticipated abandonment by her husband. Both issues converge to overwhelm her as she unconsciously inventories her own resources to cope with these extraordinary challenges.

JOAN

This record is included because it illustrates the subjective phenomenology of an experience found in a number of psychotic states; namely, conflict over the expression of anger. The patient, Joan, is a mother in her mid-thirties who became acutely psychotic in the midst of marital difficulty. She was the product of a very disturbed family in which her father, an alcoholic, was prone to violent rages and abusive treatment of his children when he was intoxicated. When sober, he was a passive recipient of denigration and sarcasm at the hands of his wife. Joan learned both to fear and to feel sorry for her father. He was, in her eyes, either terribly threatening or painfully weak. Joan grew up having learned to shrink from the aggression of others and to disown such feelings when they arose within her. In her second marriage, to a brilliant but dominating man, she experienced frequent criticism, intellectual challenge, and blame for problems that arose. She felt herself inferior and unable to meet (or question) the standards he dictated for her. Her rage returned unrecognized in the form of fantasies of violence and mutilation which she described in a series of "letters" to her physician during the early days of her hospitalization for a psychotic reaction.

Dear Doctor:

Well, my universe is broadening. It seems that through this neurosis or whatever it is, I am seeking to re-think my whole status of assumptions—that's the phrase that comes to mind. Today my husband visited and it was a long re-thinking process. I talked about early dating patterns, my lack of homosexual experience yet sympathy for the homosexual. There are lots of answers I don't have, but I am rushing myself too fast I think. My stomach's always anxious and I am in a constant state of apprehension. I wish I could just let myself slow down. Why am I in such a damn hurry. Please tell me why I am in such a damn fucking hurry to do this thing. It's like fighting to save your consciousness, back-peddling with yourself like sudden vollies shut off ("shut" for "shot"—I must keep my mouth "shut" says association) about my real lack of intention about giving any of my neurosis up for anything—even normality. Why do I want to hurt my husband? So he will reject me? I answer, OK, now I say can I get some sleep? I still need very much to be slowed down and to hear why everything is so fast . . . We (my husband and I) talked yesterday of my being a secret bourgeoise, of wanting the ring and affidavits of legalized courtship. We talked of my wanting to keep him by getting pregnant with one of the children. Then I was not aware of this, just thought vaguely of wanting his child and did not use any precautions. Back to the rings. I bought two rings in New York last July, paid a deposit on them. I don't know why I chose the rings. That they symbolized an acceptance of me I wasn't getting from him then and that there had been no rings at our marriage ceremony by law? . . . Discussion with my husband of my homosexuality or rather lack of it, that I had none of that experience in my childhood or teen-age years. The other doctor said that I was a schizophrenic. That hurt my feelings and ego picture greatly. Seems so irrevocable and utterly hopeless . . . This is what the neurosis wants to drive me to do (or I want me to do): get a complete cure of all my sexual problems before I see my husband again. You see he wants to have a "real" wife, a normal wife who responds. He wants to have nothing between us. No more saying you are having an orgasm when you are not. This is what I did for ten years but now he wants to go through the whole analysis with me vicariously. I can never say "stop" or "no" to him about thoughts. All my thoughts must be available to us for examination. Now this comes at a better time than before—the constant anxiety problem stopped last night. It was unbelievable. Now it's all gone. After all, didn't I come here to break down and to have just such things examined—my sexual problem. I am frightened. My husband says he would take me if I had no responses ever, never an orgasm. But I think he and I need more because I can't talk about it before it's cleared up to him again. Not the way we are now. We are utterly intense now. Every time I look away he says "What are you thinking?" and we go down another abyss. I think these thoughts are perhaps handled better by patient and doctor, not husband and wife. I mean, he's out there taking care of our children, folding our clothes, waiting for me to come home. Lying in bed at night and I love him. I must be able to talk to him without folding emotionally and without sounding abnormal to him. And to do so I must be normal since there can be no lying or deceit in my thoughts that we don't examine. Because I saw that looking down into myself, I would be facing those same terrors that I faced at the other hospital with suicide at the end of the path again. I *must* shed the old defenses and acquire new realistic ones to meet my inadequacies. That's not garbage—I really mean it. All that keeps me from seeing the world clearly must go. I must get well before I see him. I must not need to clobber him so, emotionally. He is going through agonies about the affair and I was unsympathetic. I had gotten too involved in myself again, I did not have a clear picture of his life at home without me, how each friend who comes in is a difficulty, how I must "re-see" each friend, each object in our house . . . Everything looks like a weapon to hurt myself with, the pencils to put out my eyes, the washing soaps in the broom closet to drink, the frame on my glasses, the glass in my glasses. When alone I reconstruct the neurosis, pretend I can have it all again, the money spending, the clothes buying, the lover. I don't want to do this. It just seems to happen. I get bullied out of being an adult, of making my own choices, of doing my own way . . . a final image of my husband with my taking a chop at his neck and of his forcing me to do something at the same time . . . The next time my husband visits may we see each other privately to talk and make love? I think (if I can be tranquilized and not acting as in my previous letter) that this would be a big help to him and me. Especially to him at home and to me here, relieving my guilt about acting in such a selfish way (going to the hospital, receiving care like a child, etc.) . . . "She's schizoid and she believes her husband has started a plot to kill her." Oh, my mind comes up with the strangest things. I want my husband and children. Please help me. Take me off the back-peddling merry-go-round, stop the rapidity of thought. I must get down to basics, am chipping slowly off some of that boulder which is the monstrous rock of my unconscious. I hope to get *back* to it soon. Meant to write *down*. The meaning is obvious, want to get "back" to my neurosis. Image of hitting my husband over the back of the neck with a grass cutter. The one that comes on a long pole for chopping low grass. God, please let me rest. I've had enough insights for awhile . . . I feel as if I had two piles of knowledge, one on each side of me. One is big, the other is small. I am between them with a cleansing tub. The big pile is full of things not exposed to my new insights. I must pick up each item and put them in the tub to cleanse them. Then and only then can they be put on the other side, the good side. This is a lot of work, I feel, and brings a great feeling of inadequacy. Will my mind take the strain or will I need shock or something? One side of me wants to work hard at this project, the other wants to relax and slip away into an unreality of irresponsibility . . . Came to the part about the lion kill in our nature—life reading selections. Made me very nervous, feel the pain of the nervous fit flow and ebb, like a tide inside me. God, you've got to help me! Feel great for one minute, then down for so long. Oh, why did this happen to me? Call off your monsters, I'll be good. Why do I say *your* monsters? Do I think you are all involved in a plot to unnerve me? Got to learn to handle reality better. Have my sons been killed? A shocking thought hits me. Now look, you can't worry about things like that. Life will go on without you even if the children had been hurt. You must not take the blame. Leave such things where they lie. You must learn to live life even if they were not there waiting for you. You must learn to love yourself. I don't feel too much love for self at this moment. Too far down. Please help bring me back. I feel as if I were on the escalator of thought, where things start going faster and faster . . . My husband will have to wait till I get better about the sex thing. He is just a baby about immediate gratification sometimes (That is my former doctor's insight, not mine. I don't believe you accuse the power in authority *openly*. No, only behind his back) . . . Image of the ghastly knitting needles, one such in ear through to brain, like the image of the killing in previews of coming attractions. God, you can't always be protected. I'll just have to get stronger. The worst anxiety comes from thoughts about razors and cut flesh (my own, sometimes the boys). Oh, how can they grow up well with such an aggressive mother. Save me from my thoughts. Afraid the illness is getting ready to clobber me . . . I am very depressed. Keep thinking that I can kill myself if I want to. I could, for instance, stick my fingers into my eyes and pull out the eyeballs like testicles, play with them like balls. Image of swinging testicles of my husband, cupping them gently, then tearing them off his body.

Comment

In the setting of a hostile, unpredictable, and unstable family of origin, this woman learned substantially to doubt her own worth and developed a strategy of avoidance in the face of exploitation by others. In marriage to a talented but controlling man, success would have required that she confidently assert and pursue her own style and interests. She was unable to oppose him in any useful way, however, fearing both her own assertiveness and the hostility which opposition provoked in her husband. In time her evasion led to activities (excessive spending, an affair) which only intensified her feelings of worthlessness. Caught in the impasse created by her wish for self-respect and individuality in the marriage versus her fear of the internal and external hostility that pursuing such goals would require, she developed an acute psychosis.

The psychotic state itself is characterized in this instance by intense anxiety, rapidity of ideational processes, and intrusive thoughts that she might harm herself or her family. The patient apparently felt that somehow in the plethora of ideas, memories, and connected thoughts lay the "key" or "answer." She was supported in this notion by her husband, a man who enjoyed "playing with" ideas, fantasies, and "associations," and who did not want to acknowledge the real desperation of his wife. Her method of dealing with the *content* of the psychotic experience is characteristic: self-denigration, striving for acceptance from her husband, and disavowal of the significance of her violent fantasies other than claiming that they were further evidence of her worthlessness. It is noteworthy that even in her psychotic state "primary process" content appears in somewhat disguised form. Her hostility thus returns grotesque and in caricature; she recoils from it but refuses to recognize its more humane, ultimately challenging and demanding significance. Thus, in the psychotic state as in dreams, crucial conflictual themes may achieve differential degrees of manifest expression at varying levels of symbolic disguise. In most instances, as the accounts illustrate, the actual experience is a complex phenomenon fashioned by an interaction between state-determined and individual-determined components. As the present account shows, characteristic defensive strategies and reactions are part of the contribution which the individual makes to psychotic experience.

CATHERINE

The next account is a final example of psychosis arising in the context of marital disharmony. Catherine had been married for seven years and was the mother of three children. From the first years of her marriage she had been aware of real incompatibilities with her husband. While a rather competent person during her adolescence, she seemed to thrive on praise for her looks and apparently developed minimal sense of herself or the course she wanted her life to take. She was the favorite of a father who was frequently, inexplicably, angry and punitive. Her marriage to a man who was taciturn and controlling, and with whom she shared few interests, was a rather impulsive act. Children came rapidly and her own needs and interests received low priority. In the later years of her marriage divorce was frequently contemplated and discussed, but the responsibilities and loneliness of this prospect were apparently too frightening. In the context of this tenuous life situation, Catherine's mother fell ill with cancer. Catherine's acute illness developed in this setting and was described by her in the following document which she wrote after she had been in the hospital approximately five weeks.

Where does this story begin. I am not sure, and who knows where it will end. I guess for a point of reference it began around Christmas of 1970 with a phone call from Paris from my sister who seemed very homesick and upset. She wanted very much for me to visit her in Rome where she was in school until the 15th of January. Although I was prepared to visit her (shots and passport) I had decided not to go as my husband wouldn't go with me, but because of Janet's extremely agitated state, I promised that I would meet her either in Paris or Rome about the third of January. Well, I went, I saw and I guess in a way, I conquered. I became myself again, interested in all things, and a part of my surroundings. In three days my sister had to leave for London to pick up a ticket to the States, so I went to London at the same time and planned to return to the States on the 15th or the same day Jan was to go home. After the Italian sunshine, the smog and foul air of London just wasn't it, so I returned to Rome alone. I had met students there and a staff member in the school in the convent who was going to help me find a place to stay either in or near the school. Why I had to return to Rome I do not really know. I wanted to get to know my way around as I believe I belong there in a way. I had long ago given up on my marriage and had planned to divorce my husband after he went to school in February and things were well in hand for him. Back in Rome, I learned to get around on my own somewhat in three more days of Italian sunshine and although I wasn't ready to leave, as I wished to know the city and people better for my next trip, I returned on the first available flight following the phone call from my husband which was an order to return immediately. Ladybug, Ladybug—Your children are with your sister-in-law and their lives are falling apart.

During all of this trip I felt very close to God, very happy, and I thought a lot about my life and prayed in the garden of the convent for love, wisdom, happiness, etc., and for a man with whom I could share life and love. All the things I had prayed for as a child. One afternoon, in the garden, I looked up to see a statue of Jesus in a "suffer little children to come unto me" pose with hand outstretched. He seemed to be calling to me—saying come here and kneel at my feet. My heart was open to God but I was too proud to kneel so I stood at the base of the statue. And as it has since seemed, a miracle happened. My life was given to me again—new, but with all of the lessons I had already learned still there. Perhaps it was the next day or the day after—a Monday—on which I went to the airport—two hours by bus, to return to Connecticut. At the ticket counter I saw a man—a very rare man—standing in my line of sight quietly. I thought somewhere was a very happy woman. As it turned out he identified with me as much as I with him. He was a widower with three children who said "Do you have a great belief in God?" and when I answered "Yes" he said, "Then believe that God meant for us to meet." This man spoke to me in similes and while I thought I understood what he meant when he answered my question "What is your second favorite hobby" with a simple and modest "You'll think this presumptious, but Life," I have since wondered about this answer. As to me he gave Life and Love. A new Life and God's love.

After we landed in New York, he said he could

not let me walk away and he had already asked me to go to Rome with him in two days. He offered to find a hotel for me and drive me home the next day as I was not feeling well. Coming home was very upsetting for me but I refused his kindness and went back to my home. As a goodbye, he kissed me lightly on the lips and left to return in a few moments and put a cross on my forehead, bless me and kiss my cheek.

The trip from Rome to my home took in all about 17 hours, and 24 hours of wakefulness before I was able to get some rest because of the social amenities involved in returning. The next morning I was up before the sun, still being on Rome time, and was for the rest of the week. I discovered that home shared the same sun as Rome and that it wasn't where one was but what one was that made the difference. I was me, the real me. No more pretending I could make a marriage from a terribly lonely existence which had lasted for seven years. No more praying to be strong enough to take only responsibility for my life until my children were independent enough so that I could start life over. Jesus or rather God had given me a promise of a new life through Jesus and John, the man I had met. But as I told John when I called him two days later to say goodbye, this was something I had to do entirely on my own. My decisions had to be the same decisions I would have to have if I had never met him, the same truth had to apply to my life as had applied before. No involvements for this Chick (new words, now words, for me, not then words).

The first two days at home were a nightmare. My husband, who had always been insanely jealous, and who had questioned me many times before, sometimes all night about my fidelity stuck to me like glue, monitored the telephone and questioned me incessantly about the affairs with every name he found in my address book. Even one girl named Billy. He told me that a boy named Ed had called me from Rome when I returned from the drugstore on the second day of my trial, and it was a lie to test my reaction to this information. He searched my pocketbook three times that I know of, and put me through every emotion known to man, or in this case perhaps woman is a better word . . . My stomach tied itself up in knots, I lost 15 pounds in three days and I was unable to eat until I promised myself I would call a lawyer on Thursday afternoon . . . This decision gave me such a feeling of relief that I ate something for the first time on Thursday evening. Friday, when I began to procrastinate about the lawyer, my stomach again started screaming to me, so I called the lawyer and spoke to him for a while. Once more I called for legal orientation before I finally broke down and visited the lawyer to speak seriously about a divorce, custody, settlement, etc., and legal separation. My lawyer advised me that my husband sounded psychotic and that I had grounds for a divorce (mental cruelty) and he advised me to have papers drawn up immediately as I was in pretty bad shape and I would be best off to be alone for awhile to recreate myself.

I followed his advice until I tried to discuss the divorce with my husband, and he appeared to be cracking. I felt strong and sure of what I was doing. I had no intention of cracking, so I tried to help him. He promised to see a marriage counselor with me, and I felt that the least this would accomplish would be for us to understand what had happened so we wouldn't make the same mistakes twice and the most it would accomplish would be to quiet the otherwise inevitable courtroom hassle. So for another month I tried to be strong, I tried to help my husband, and I tried not to lose myself in the day to day routine of living with someone whom I did not care for in the way a woman must care for a man.

During this time I had a lot of love for my children and sometime somehow they had come to know God. They taught me a great deal and I loved them more than I ever had before, and I was very proud of them. However, as Shakespeare said, a wise father knows his own son, but my husband does not know them.

During this time many new experiences were mine. I shall try to explain. Perhaps it would be relevant to say also at this point that I was dreaming again. I had not dreamt for a long time. Also I felt like a woman—my hormones were running around like they were supposed to. My figure improved a little and all in all I was healthier than I had been for a very long time. I attribute these things to the effect of being loved or feeling love.

My mother called about Friday to ask about the trip. She sounded great and I forgot for the time being that the doctor had only given her six months to live. Barring miracles. I wanted to tell her about this man I met as I felt she would be happy for me, but I was not sure and I didn't want to upset her so I kept my secret. The next day she was returned to the hospital. I learned about it on Sunday morning, and Sunday evening I took a nap and had a nightmare. In my dream I was asked to give my life for my mother and I refused. I felt she had lived as she had chosen and my life was mine to live as I chose. I couldn't give it up for anyone except for God.

I had two more strange dreams or whatever they were. They were more like trances or something as I felt powerless to get out of them although I struggled very hard to wake up. The second dream a couple of days later—I was climbing a yellow carpeted stairway. A woman dressed in red was at the top and my children were at the bottom calling to me. I could not go up without them and I wasn't sure that I wanted to climb these stairs anyway, but I felt that I had to so I lay down somewhere in the middle and called out aloud to my son. He heard me and came upstairs and answered me and it woke me from the dream. My husband also heard me and thought that I was calling to him. I told him that I had a very strange nightmare and I was frightened. He was kind to me and tried to help me relax. Two decisions—two dreams.

The third dream was an empty dream. I heard again as in the second a strange noise and my mind was a total blank. I thought I was losing control of my mind and I was scared. My mind seemed to be expanding and when I came out of it, I wondered if somewhere along the line someone had slipped me some LSD as I imagined that this must be the kind of effect one would have after taking a drug. I have never taken drugs.

During the time I was home I began to read my Bible. I knew God would help me to straighten out my problems. I wanted to know exactly what the Bible had to say about divorce and other questions. I sought wisdom and truth. Seek and ye shall find, knock and it shall be opened unto you. I sought, I found a great deal and yet I knew there was more. Even now I know there is more, but I think I will not be part of the rest. My mind became a sponge. I read philosophy for enlightenment and found only echoes of my own mind and thoughts. I decided the Bible was the real book and others were other men's living of what the Bible told. My reading list was something like this: Nietsche, Kahlil Gibran, Herman Hesse, and other books and modern prophets. I never completed my reading as my books got left behind when I was sent to the hospital but I found these books entertaining, enjoyable and funny. Echoes of my mind.

All of life on earth related to me. Music had meaning, all music, and the meaning was life, and life was mine. I began exercising and later I found that the exercises were Yoga. I prayed a lot for guidance from God and he helped me. Each new book led to many more books and I began quitting the books in the middle somewhere as I didn't have time to finish them. Dante's "Paradiso" remains unfinished. In my mind Beatrice corresponded to John and the "Who are you" was the exact phrase I used. The answer had been a simple "A man who sat next to you on an airplane." And yet it was much more and many people had sat next to me. This was the first man I had ever met. A man who had suffered great sorrow and loss and who could love life because he knew the meaning of living.

The cross on my forehead began to grow heavy. I could feel the lines in my forehead and occasionally I would trace them when I thought of John. I felt close to him even though he was at least 4,000 miles away. His love was a day to day part of my life. Now things began to happen. I knew my sisters as I never had before. I came to know my neighbor and closest friend. She understood what was happening to me. And I know my mother, a lioness, the mother of a lioness, who was fighting every day for a life I thought she had given up on many years before. The cross on my forehead had a seal over it, a wooden cross with a seal. Then the large white wings were put over the seal. I tried to find the meaning of these signs. I felt God was calling to me to some work which I had been born to do and the time was now. The age of Aquarius, the time for the second coming of Christ. I was going to John and I promised myself to him and to God. But I couldn't leave my children behind, even though they knew God and I knew that they would always know him.

I felt very strongly that I had the power to heal. I finally decided to help my mother if she wanted to live and I held out my right hand and drew her illness (cancer) from her stomach. The next day I went to visit her. Again I (while staying at my husband's parents) held out my hand to draw my mother's illness from her. The next day when I visited my mother in the hospital she said she felt the tumor in her stomach shrinking. I couldn't believe this was true. I said nothing except that she looked strong and that I loved her. Still she had cancer in her lungs and the doctor thought in her heart as she had a heart beat of 200 for three hours one morning. Still it was a matter that she could die any day barring miracles . . I happen to believe in miracles.

On a Friday evening after I had promised myself to John and God I began to feel that time was getting short. That the time for learning was over and time for action was near. Time was too short. I was not wise, only learning. Decisions had to be made and I could only, eventually, trust in God as His way is true and right. So I gave up my decisions to God eventually and prayed for help.

Friday evening my daughter stood on the edge of

the tub, held out her arms and said, "Mommy I forgot the word." I asked innocently, "What word?" She said, "Oh now I know," and said, "Master" as she leaped off the edge of the tub. Pearls of wisdom out of the mouths of babes.

I knew that I was postponing, procrastinating. But I felt that for the sake of my husband and the kids I had to do what I could to keep things in hand. Unfortunately for me I tried too hard to make the divorce easy for my husband. I cracked, broke, whatever . . .

Now I have to start over again. Back to my lawyer's advice to get legal separation (have divorce papers drawn up) and get away for a little while if I can afford it. My mother is home from the hospital. The day I cracked, I left in the middle of the early A.M. to visit her as I was afraid she would die before I could see her. I drove East into the rising sun and arrived about seven A.M. She wasn't surprised to see me so early. I told her I loved her and hugged her and felt confident that she would be okay. Then I drove around for awhile unsure of where to go and what to do next. I wanted to see a minister but didn't know one well enough to see him so early.

Finally I went to my dad's house, had breakfast, and brought my books in to read from the car. I had a feeling that this was my judgment day, the day of my final test. My faith in God was being tested on this day, and it was, and I proved true to God's love. I felt that the sun could not set on me in my husband's house, because I had vowed myself to God. I was not well, I started hemorrhaging Saturday night perhaps because I took one birth control pill, then was sorry that I had, so I didn't take the next 20. I went back home through very bad driving weather to take my children with me. They are usually with me and I want and love them very much. I could not take them. My husband would not allow it and he wouldn't let me out again. I thought he and the children would be harmed as a punishment for me if I did not go. I felt very strange like I must go out and be away from my husband but he wouldn't let me out of the door.

I collapsed on the floor after yelling "Do you want to die" and "They are killing me." My voice was not mine, it was someone else saying "They are killing me," and it was because of me that someone I felt this close to was dying. My husband finally opened the door and I went out to the car. I was in terrible pain and hemorrhaging. I thought I was dying. The ambulance came to bring me to the hospital. I placed my hand on my stomach and gradually I became better. I don't know how long I was in the hospital but when my husband came near me the panic and sense of dying returned so I screamed at him to go away and leave me alone. No doctor saw me while I was there except Dr. Smith who came about midnight. When he sat by the bed I immediately felt better as though by holding up his hand or just looking at me he had taken away my illness. He brought me to this hospital and had my husband drive the car and as long as Dr. Smith was there it was okay. I felt somehow that he was protecting me and I was glad for his presence. He was a shepherd to me and I a little lost lamb. This hospital frightened me for the first couple of days and to that I attribute the rest of my strange behavior. Now I feel well in hand and about ready to straighten out my life.

172 RETREAT FROM SANITY

Comment

This patient's marriage had fostered a continuation of
adolescent dependency upon a controlling parental figure at the expense of her own aspirations for continued
growth and fulfillment. Hope for a more gratifying life
was held in check by her own needs for support and care.
The mother's illness apparently upset the balance and
revived the challenge of the conflict between security and
self-development. This account therefore illustrates the
manner in which life events and developmental demands
may specifically revive and test out certain character liabilities of long standing, producing developmental impasse which determines the timing of psychotic illness.

The state-determined aspects of her experience assumed a "psychedelic" form.

> My mind seemed to be expanding and when I
> came out of it I wondered if somewhere along
> the line someone had slipped me some LSD . . .
> My mind became a sponge. I read philosophy
> for enlightenment and found only echoes of
> my own mind and thoughts . . . All of life on
> earth related to me. Music had meaning, all
> music, and the meaning of life, and life was
> mine . . . I knew my sisters as I never had be-
> fore. I came to know my neighbor and closest
> friend.

We recognize the familiar enhanced sense of personal
meaning of external and internal perceptual data. The
content of the experience which pours forth in the altered state suggests the specific conflicts with which she
is contending.

> No more pretending I could make a marriage
> from a terribly lonely existence which had

lasted for seven years . . . I wanted to know exactly what the Bible had to say about divorce
and other questions . . . But I couldn't leave my
children behind even though they knew God
and I knew that they would always know Him
. . . The time for learning was over and the
time for action was near . . . I was not wise,
only learning . . . I felt that he [doctor] was
protecting me and I was glad for his presence.
He was a shepherd to me and I a little lost
lamb.

In this same regard, her dreams similarly reflect the
conflict which her mother's imminent death and the
prospects of divorce produced when measured alongside
her own desires for security and a more gratifying life. As
noted previously, her delusional resolution of the conflict is wishful and premature. Nevertheless it seems
reasonable to assume that future therapy will have to
take into account her progressive desire for growth as
well as her avoidance of the effort and pain which genuine growth will require.

The three accounts presented in this chapter illustrate
the experiential structure of psychoses which have arisen
within the context of marriage. In all three instances the
writers had married extremely controlling husbands
with powerful dependency needs of their own, only thinly veiled by their authoritarian behavior. These husbands shared certain characteristics with the fathers of
these women, who were remembered as capriciously aggressive and intimidating. The fathers had fostered a
kind of fearful compliance in their daughters and, curiously, the daughters had perpetuated that interaction
by their choices of husbands. At what level of patterning

or motivation such choices were made is difficult to say with certainty. For it appears that unconfident young women like these may be attracted by the "hard sell" suitor whose forcefulness and domination they mistake for manliness and competence. Such women seek strong external sources of self-confirmation; their goals in marriage are to recreate and rework the human constellations of their original families. They are poor and reticent judges of male character and potential. In time, a husband's own needs and deficiencies become more evident and may be exacerbated by the arrival of children. A wife's desire for personal growth thus becomes progressively thwarted by internal and external constraints. Neither partner initially appreciated or conveyed the degree to which they needed marriage for the satisfaction of strong human needs based upon a parent-child model.

Themes related to unmet dependency needs are thus encountered in the experiential fabric of psychoses arising in this context. For example, infantile rage may surge into psychotic consciousness in overt or disguised form, as we have seen. Experiences of childhood may be vividly recalled in great detail and wishful fantasies may create the illusion that strong, supportive objects are in fact available. Psychoses occurring in the context of marriage invariably indicate that the dependency needs brought to the relationship by both partners are greater than the coalition can gratify.

8. Experiential Progression in Acute Psychosis

In preceding chapters we have examined the timing, form, and content of psychotic experience as revealed through accounts obtained from individual patients. In the present chapter, utilizing these and other records, we will construct a composite picture of the experiential sequences in acute psychotic reactions. As a general model, this formulation will not be completely comprehensive; nevertheless, it will serve to highlight the temporal progression of processes we have been emphasizing in the individual accounts.

The study of consciousness is frustrating. Though we utilize each day a basic faith that our experience is closely akin to that of our fellows, it is categorical that we can never demonstrate scientifically that we are in fact observing another's conscious experience. We can ask ("What are you thinking?" or "What were you feeling?"), but we can never be sure of the validity of the report. Yet we proceed operationally in all phases of human encounter, and we act on the notion that we can, for purposes of living, come close to understanding the experience of another. There are ways of refining this approach. One can go over and over an experience with someone, attempting alternately to live through the eyes of the other person and then to step back, look for inconsistencies, improbabilities, and ambiguities. In essence one uses his own experience and his capacity to empathize to get at the experience of another. At best this is an impure, approximate form of knowing; yet it can be important and fruitful if one is able to accept avenues of investigation which are not scientifically pure in order to get at experiences which are distinctively human.

Fifteen patients, ages 20 to 38, were studied in the hospital over periods of from six weeks to three months following their first admission for an acute psychotic reaction, meaning here simply an acute delusional process with no known organic or toxic cause and usually treated with antipsychotic drugs. In these individuals, rather rapid remission of psychotic symptoms often allowed detailed investigation with the patient regarding his experience of the illness. Individual patients were seen in interviews (usually three or four), and were asked to give their own account of the onset and progression of their experience. Patients were asked qualifying questions such as "What did you think was happening?," "How did you explain that to yourself?," etc. From these interviews a composite picture of the progression of the experience of acute psychosis was obtained.

The timing of the acute psychotic reaction is of particular interest, and we have considered this issue in some detail previously. We have pointed to the way in which the confluence of individual liability or trait, developmental task and current circumstance (including drug use) interact to influence timing in acute psychosis. Patients often initially said that "It came out of the blue;" however, on further questioning one could essentially always discover a state of mind characterized by conflict and impasse. Such phrases as "I had nowhere to turn," "There was no way out," were common. Often the basic emotional state was one of intense dread as a crucial maturational step was confronted but retreated from because of overwhelming guilt or fear of abandonment. Life-threatening conflict was perceived, but neither "flight" nor "fight" seemed possible. Rapid oscillations in mood were common. Sometimes this impasse was displaced to an intellectual concern, as in the two following examples in which the essential intrapsychic conflict is only thinly disguised.

Example 1—A 23-year-old nurse graduate student was preparing a thesis proposal around the time of her acute psychotic disruption. She had been raised in a very sheltered family in the Midwest. Immediately prior to her admission she had become rather intimately involved with two different men; this experience had forced serious rethinking of her sexual attitudes. In addition, she had simultaneously been involved in a "T-group" experience which stressed "being yourself." Questions about her role and feelings as a woman were frequently raised in therapy subsequently. A rough draft of the thesis proposal (a manual for breast feeding) contained the following statements:

This researcher feels that the mother needs support in her decision to breast feed and a basic understanding of how to do it. If a mother is motivated to breast feed, it is her right as an individual to do it, and it is the responsibility of those who know how to help her, to give her the help . . . perhaps the reason they can't really help her is because they make her feel she shouldn't have the right to do what she wants because they feel they can't . . . the confidence is based on the fact that the mother is a woman who has the facilities to breast feed and then assumes she can. However, the mother will quickly lose this confidence when she finds that there can be obstacles to breast feeding if she doesn't know what to do with them. When a mother decides how to feed her baby, she needs confidence that she can do it, and her ability to do it demonstrates that she knows how and so has reason for her confidence.

Example 2—A 21-year-old male undergraduate was involved in an intimate relationship with a woman, his first, just prior to his admission for acute psychosis. He had also been exploring a number of other new activities, such as drinking, of which he felt his parents would disapprove. At the same time he was writing what was to him a very important paper on "musical nationalism." Six weeks after admission he spoke of this paper as follows:

> I spent the summer thinking about my nationalism paper. If my concept of nationalism is correct, it has implications for 19th century romanticism, much of which needs revising. According to some sources this is all that happened in the 19th century. But somehow the old concept didn't take care of all the facts. The old boundaries couldn't handle all the material. In addition to nationalism and romanticism, there was also liberalism and individualism. I was trying to feel my way through a whole body of material which had been largely unexplored.

Both of these examples of "displacement" of the pre-psychotic conflict graphically depict the contending intrapsychic forces. In the first an outgrown, apologetic feminine self-concept confronts a more positive, self-as-

sured sense of womanhood. In the second a rigid, op-
pressive, personal morality faces the expanding experience of late adolescence. Ronald Laing[1] has described the
existential predicament of the "divided self" in the prepsychotic individual, and a similar picture of conflict
within their own mental self-representation was described in retrospect by most of the patients whose accounts we have previously examined.

THE DESTRUCTURING OF PERCEPTION AND AFFECT

The Experience of Heightened Awareness

From the experience of impasse, patients often but not
invariably proceeded to an experience of heightened
awareness. It was sometimes difficult to catch this transition before the onset of true delusions, yet it was clear-
cut in some instances. This kind of experience was discussed in a previous chapter and noted in several patients' records. It is actually similar to one which many
people have at times of acute crisis or "peak" life experience. There is a feeling of inexpressible urgency.
The need for sleep seems to lessen and insomnia often
sets in unnoticed. There is a sense that something is
about to happen. Visual and auditory sensation may
seem particularly acute. Thoughts and perceptions come
faster than they can be assimilated. At such times individuals may feel that their minds have awakened, that
they are functioning at a high level, or that their creative
powers are enhanced. They may experience emotions
with singular intensity and often are overcome with a
sense of benevolence or overwhelming fear. Memories of
childhood and long-forgotten emotions or emotionally
colored events may surge into consciousness. Some patients reported temporarily enhanced sexual feeling. It is

as if the barriers to inner and outer sensations have been removed and the individual confronts raw experience in the here and now as well as from his own particular intrapsychic past.

In addition to the sense of heightened awareness to inner and outer stimuli, there is frequently a temporarily heightened sense of self. Erikson[2] has noted that identity is an experience as well a psychological construct. He further states that there are periods of extreme identity consciousness, that "We are thus most aware of our identity when we are just about to gain it . . . or when we are just about to enter a crisis and feel the encroachment of identity diffusion." The following description of heightened awareness, written in retrospect by a young student admitted for acute psychosis, demonstrates most of the characteristics of this altered state of consciousness.

One night I woke up and started feeling good again. I felt I could do more with my time, that anything was possible. I felt alive and vital, full of energy. My senses seemed alive, colors were very bright, they hit me harder. Things appeared clear-cut, I noticed things I had never noticed before. There was a feeling of exhilaration, a sense of union with the whole world. Time slowed down, much more experience could be crowded into a brief time span. Sexually I felt awakened, competent, responsive. I seemed to notice symmetry and harmony, and I wanted to experience everything. I could concentrate on a speck of something and just stare at it. A whole new world opened up, and I felt more secure than ever before. I felt like an individual, that I had found my identity which had always been like patchwork before. I saw individuality in others now, and I enjoyed having differences.

Ideas of Reference and Influence

Not only is the pace of experience for the incipient psychotic frequently heightened, it is also qualitatively altered. Things seem to have hidden meanings, neutral individuals are suddenly animated with strange ideas and designs, curious connections between feelings and perception are experienced. Categories of relevance, normally capable of sifting experience automatically, are broadened. Everything experienced is measured as to its possible relevance for the individual. Most non-psychotic individuals can recall times of acute crisis in which every sound, every newcomer was processed intrapsychically with regard to his relevance for the crisis at hand. This phenomenon can be seen teleologically as serving a useful function, for at times of mortal danger (real or assumed), the organism is geared to scrutinize the entire perceptual field. For the incipient psychotic the suspicion or possibility of relevance soon proceeds to the "idea of reference," perhaps the cardinal characteristic of psychotic experience. We wish to emphasize that this shift is not intellectual but experiential. The individual literally has the irrefutable cognitive experience that this or that object, person, event, or transaction has meaning for him. Talking with individuals about this stage soon convinces one that this process is an overwhelmingly convincing one. It cannot be argued away. Categories of relevance have simply broadened in these individuals' experiences prior to the formation and systematization of meaning (delusions). The individual experiences the subsequent "press for meaning" as extraordinarily intense. Normal strictures of what is logical, reasonable, and probable fall before the onslaught of this state of increased input and disarticulated categories of relevance. Usually the experiencing self identifies the proper source of experience (feeling and ideation from within, sensory data from without). We know from common experience that these systems influence each other. Feelings and ideas can alter perceptual experience of the world, and what we perceive in the world can alter internal experience. Indeed, it is obvious from such important human capacities as motivation toward and gratification from certain types of experience, that an interplay exists between ideation, affect, and perception. In incipient psychosis it is as if the usually functioning adaptive distance between these systems has been altered, and they have become blended or merged. Seemingly, distortions can occur experientially in either direction. For instance, inner experience can distort the external world (projection). This phenomenon is operative in individuals who "project" certain personal feeling states, conflicts, or thoughts onto other people or other issues. (See clinical examples illustrating "The Setting.") As another example (described by an articulate schizophrenic[3]), one can disown as "out there" one's own "thoughts out loud" and experience auditory hallucinations. Or, finally, one can actually transform sensory reality, as in Capgras's syndrome where the experience of variable feelings directed toward or received from an individual leads to the belief that there are "doubles" or that people are "switching."[4] These processes can, of course, reach conscious levels as seen in certain psychotic patients who feel they can, by conscious effort, hypnotize or influence the thinking of others or that they themselves have been hypnotized or invaded by the thoughts of others. We have noted examples of these mechanisms in some of the patient accounts. All of these phenomena can be seen as instances in which inner experience can seriously distort and contaminate perception of the external world. The reverse is also seen. The phenomenon of synesthesia, seen in natural psychoses and drug-induced states, is an experience whereby data from one sensory modality (audition) can alter that from another (vision) or can strongly influence feeling states. The following example illustrates this two-way contamination of inner feeling states and external reality. This 23-year-old man was hospitalized shortly following his marriage. After six weeks in the hospital he related the following:

> Before my marriage, I was bothered by premature ejaculation. I tried to control this by developing my lower abdominal muscles. I became aware that my sexual ability was related to a burning sensation in my lower back. When this sensation was in front, in my loins, I felt like a totally different person, a real man. I worked for a man named Butch who was a very strong person. When Butch made certain movements with his feet I could feel the burning sensation move into my loins. I really thought that should happen with my father, but it never did. When these things are in the right place I feel whole and vibrant inside, there is something there to push me. It is a pleasure to look at someone else's eyes, feel healthy yourself, and see a healthy gaze in their eyes. I know this burning feeling inside me did happen and was affected by other people.

Thus, in acute psychosis the idea of reference or influence is an experience in which categories of experiential relevance are expanded due to several interacting processes. First, overwhelming anxiety seems to lead to hypervigilance and increased sensory scanning. Secondly, ideation and perception, normally somewhat interdependent at an adaptive level, tend to cross-contaminate each other and lead to idea-induced reality distortion or reality-induced alterations in the experiential self. This second process, tied as it is to individual experience, contributes further to the irrefutable quality of the idea of reference or influence.

THE DESTRUCTURING OF THE SENSE OF SELF

The Experience of Identity Dissolution

Almost invariably the previously described feeling of a heightened sense of self gives way to the experience of a progressive loss of the sense of self. Identity diffusion, as described by Erikson, refers to a rather gradual psychosocial process. However, in acute psychosis the loss of the immediate ongoing sense of self (mental self-representation) can often assume dramatic and bizarre proportions, as illustrated in several preceding chapters. Another illustrative example is that of a 26-year-old medical student who, at the time of my interview, had been in the hospital for three weeks because of an acute psychotic reaction. Describing the first day of hospitalization, he said:

> I had the idea that I didn't know who I was and I had to find out. I kept looking at the patients in my room to find out which one I looked like. I saw the bad side of each of them and became convinced this was the side I was similar to. I tried on other people's clothes. I said to myself, "If his clothes fit you then you must be like him." The next morning I felt okay, I knew I was _____ [Name], that I was a doctor in training, so I put on a white coat.

Having described other instances of altered self-experiences in the first chapter, we simply wish to reemphasize that in the acute psychotic experience the normally functioning and automatized mental self-representation often gives way.

The Formation of Delusions

Delusion formation has been classically considered to be a restitutive process. So it seems to be (teleologically speaking), but this view gives us no clues as to the experiential sequences involved. The foregoing consideration of the predelusional experience in incipient psychosis and the patient accounts suggest that delusions are understandable constructs derived from experiences of heightened and altered sensory influx and self-experience, widened categories of relevance, and a push for closure or meaning centering around certain intrapsychic themes. It is apparent that for the acutely psychotic individual, prior learning about "reality" has little voice once the process of delusion formation has set in.

A young man, a Ph.D. in psychology and a third-year medical student, developed an acute psychotic reaction and was able to give the following account of stages in the process of delusion formation. His experience is cited because of the insight it provides into the details of the formation and maintenance of delusional ideas in acute psychosis. This student had been experiencing extreme emotional lability as well as the haunting notion that there was something very wrong with him, that he might be going to die, that he could not breathe. One morning, after spending a fear-ridden night during which he slept little, he recounted later (author's italics):

I got up at 7 a.m., dressed, and drove to the hospital. I felt my breathing trouble might be due to an old heart lesion. I had been told when I was young that I had a small ventricular septal defect. I decided that I was in heart failure and that people felt I wasn't strong enough to accept this, so they weren't telling me. *I thought about all the things that had happened recently that could be interpreted in that light.* I looked up heart failure in a textbook and found that the section had been removed, so I concluded someone had removed it to protect me. *I remembered other comments.* A friend had talked about a "walkie talkie," and the thought occurred to me that I might be getting medicine without my knowledge perhaps by radio. I remembered someone talking about a one-way plane ticket; to me that meant a trip to Houston and a heart operation. I remembered an unusual smell in the lab and thought that might be due to the medicine they were giving me in secret. I began to think I might have a machine inside of me which secreted medicine into my blood stream. Again I reasoned that I had a disease no one could tell me about and was getting medicine for it secretly. At this point, I panicked and tried to run away, but the attendant in the parking lot seemed to be making a sign to motion me back. I thought I caught brief glimpses of a friend and my wife so I decided to go back into the hospital. A custodian's eyes attracted my attention; they were especially large and piercing. He looked very powerful. He seemed to be "in on it," maybe he was giving medicine in some way. Then I began to have the feeling that other people were watching me. And, as periodically happened throughout the early stages, *I said to myself that the whole thing*

*was absurd, but when I looked again the people
really were watching me.* I felt that comments made
in the elevator pertained to me. One patient said,
"They have the full strength medicine around
here." I thought maybe the heart medicine I was
being given was morphine and that I might get addicted. When I was in pediatric clinic there was a
conversation between the pediatric social worker
and a surgeon. He said that an operation had been
planned but the equipment was all smashed. I
thought this supported the idea that there was a
machine inside of me, and the amphetamines I had
taken messed it up. All of a sudden I felt a warm
glow. I felt these people were trying to help me.
They seemed to be giving me helpful hints. I
thought that all the doctors in a meeting I went to
were psychiatrists and that they were trying to help
me. Conversations had hidden meanings. *When
someone told me later that I was delusional,
though, I seemed to know it. But I was really groping to understand what was going on. There was a
sequence with my delusions: first panic, then groping, then elation at having found out. Involvement
with the delusions would fade in and out.* One moment I would feel I certainly didn't believe these
things; then, without realizing it, I would be caught
up in them again. When reality started coming
back, when I realized where I was and what had
happened, I became depressed. There were times
when I was aware, in a sense, that I was acting on a
delusion. One part of me seemed to say, "Keep your
mouth shut, you know this is delusion and it will
pass." *But the other side of me wanted the delusion,
preferred to have things this way.* The experience
was a passive one; that is, I just sat back as these

things happened to me. Getting better was passive too; it just happened, so to speak, as I watched.

From experiences such as this one and others, a sequence of events in the formation of delusions is suggested. (1) Impasse, dread, and overwhelming anxiety; (2) altered experience of self and world (as described above); (3) press for "making sense" of the experience; (4) overcoming of constraints imposed by normal reality guards; and (5) a certain relief and comfort (even elation) experienced with the delusional idea. Apparently, a whole series of interactions between the individual self and its altered perception of the world are required for the formation of delusional experience; in addition, a variety of ego functions or lack of them (as previously suggested for the psychedelic experience) are involved in the stepwise formation and maintenance of the delusional system.

The theoretical heritage of this work stems from the unique contributions of Paul Federn, and it seems appropriate to outline his ideas here. Federn took seriously the universal fact of ego *Erlebnis,* or ego experience, and utilized phenomenological observations to significantly modify existing psychoanalytic theories of psychosis. Whereas Freud had theorized that psychoses were characterized by an enhanced investment of the ego with mental energy consequent upon withdrawal from reality, Federn insisted that the ego in psychosis was defective and weakened. Current psychotherapeutic activities with psychotics rely heavily upon this notion. Federn felt that ego boundary cathexis was weakened in psychosis, the normal ability of the individual to take distance from or usefully to employ the unconscious, to distinguish ideation from reality, and to respond selectively to external sensation was impaired. He was undoubtedly influenced

by the Bleulerian concept of the "thought disorder," and
devoted remarkably little attention to the role of individual conflict in psychotic experience. Implicit in his theories, however, was the idea that in the psychoses a number of automatized ego functions underwent a kind of
depatterning, leading to an altered *form* of conscious
experience.

More recently, students of the phenomenology of psychosis have emphasized the personal side, the existential
pain, of the psychotic experience. R. D. Laing has been a
major protagonist for approaching psychosis from the
philosophical-existentialist viewpoint. He deplores the
dehumanizing aspects of conventional clinical terminology and calls for a new "science of persons." His thesis
proceeds from a descriptive, intuitive, and philosophical
analysis of the "self system," and his goal is to understand in emphathic terms the patient's style of being in
the world. In the United States, Adolf Meyer and Harry
Stack Sullivan were responsible for initial efforts to understand psychotic patients from the viewpoint of individual developmental psychology. Searles, basing his
observations upon extraordinarily prolonged psychotherapeutic relationships with psychotic patients, discusses their tendency to confuse feeling and outer reality
from the viewpoint of pathological interpersonal development, focusing particularly upon family attitudes in
the growth and maintenance of reliable anchoring
points for the experience of self and external world.[5]
Otto Will and Donald Burnham, also in the tradition of
Meyer and Sullivan, develop a similar position.[6/7] Stein
approaches the problem of the psychotic individual's
view of his world from a strictly philosophical viewpoint, but ends up very close to Searles and Laing in his
conclusions.[8] Thus the psychological-philosophical tradition has tended to account for both the form and con-

tent of psychotic experience as deriving from the vicissitudes of individual development.

Chapman and McGhie have studied the subjective world of the psychotic from the viewpoint of cognitive disorganization.[9] Their studies initially described and catalogued the various kinds of altered cognitive experience in psychosis, with minimal consideration of personal, existential, and developmental aspects. They focused upon sensory overstimulation, defects in attention, and word-finding difficulties in their patients. More recently, Freeman, with McGhie and Cameron, presented extensive material toward the development of a comprehensive theory of psychosis, a theory which would account both for an altered state of consciousness as well as individual-specific dynamic themes and content. Focusing upon the concept of impaired object relations in psychotic states, these authors integrated their observations of disordered cognition in these conditions into an overall psychoanalytic framework.[10]

Silverman[11] and Livingston and Blum[12] have tested experimentally the notion that schizophrenic patients overscan but derive minimal, or idiosyncratic, meaning from their perceptual world. Deikman,[13] while not working with psychotic patients, has studied experiential alterations as a consequence of experimental meditation. He has shown that meditation itself can result in a number of alterations in perception of self and external world. His notion of deautomatization of ego functions seems consonant with Federn's ideas, though Deikman carefully specifies those ego functions which become altered and details the process of alteration through meditation.

Thus a consideration of experiential progression in acute psychosis seems to strengthen the basic psychoanalytic tenet that the development of cognitive skills occurs

in an affective milieu. Affective, ideational and perceptual experience undergo simultaneous and interrelated
regression (unmasking of developmentally earlier affective and perceptual modes) in acute psychosis. The progression of the psychotic state and the formation of delusions is favored by the presence of this altered state, plus
the absence of certain corrective ego functions. Further,
we might speculate about the unique defects in prepsychotic individuals which allow the acute psychotic reaction to develop. Initially, we could postulate a defect
which allows the development of psychological impasse.
Prepsychotic individuals seem incapable of deciding and
acting at crucial developmental times in such a way as to
resolve impasse. They lack the ability to be efficacious, to
negate the world or others at crucial times of doubt or
dread.[14] Whether this inability to engage objects for the
solution of developmental impasse is primary (a defect
in initiative or social "tropism," and hence part of a
more pervasive primary defect in the acquisition of
meaningful human relations) or secondary (due to a
learned fear of others, i.e., because of a persistently intrusive, overwhelming parent) is not clear. Indeed a low anxiety threshold or defect in exploratory drive as a basic
neurobiological trait would undoubtedly play a determining role in social learning and be operative at crucial
developmental points. Secondly, we must account for
the fact that—given the experience of overwhelming
dread—the unique altered state which characterizes psychotic experience supervenes. Some kind of inherent or-
ganismic bias to such alterations in consciousness—a
unique "end-organ" liability—is certainly suggested.
Third, once the depatterning of experience of self and
world has begun, prepsychotics seem unable to stem the
tide. Many "normal" individuals can recall near-psy-
chotic experiences (often at crucial maturational pe-

riods) from which they have literally torn themselves away. Finally, once psychotic experiencing has taken hold, these individuals seem curiously unable (or unwilling) to bring prior knowledge of reality to bear for correcting their experiences. Thus the psychotic experience itself can provide a kind of shelter from emotional pain and the demands of reality which may not be easily put aside. By this analysis we suggest that both "nature" and "nurture" must be understood, not as parallel, but as interacting processes, if we are to comprehend the timing, form, content, and progression of psychotic human experience.

9. *Psychosis and Human Development*

INTRODUCTION

In previous chapters we have suggested that acute psychoses occur initially at periods of developmental impasse as crucial growth tasks are being confronted. In this chapter we will examine this notion in greater detail. At least two ideas seem to be crystallizing from much of the current clinical research dealing with psychotic states. First is the notion that current terminology is in great need of revision. Much of our Kraepelinian and Bleulerian heritage has been tested and found wanting.[1] Experience suggests that current diagnostic labels in psychosis have neither test-retest reliability nor predictive value. Rare studies of the natural history of psychosis demonstrate that intra-individual diagnostic variation over a period of years can span the list of most traditional subtypes.[2] Currently we are only beginning to attempt to account for the *course* of psychotic illness rather than to utilize static categories.

The other emerging (more properly, re-emerging) observation is that some psychotic patients recover and go on to progress psychologically and socially; that is, continue to develop as human beings. Recent workers have attempted to explain this fact by emphasizing various premorbid social factors which appear related to level of cognitive and perceptual functioning and to prognosis.[3] Such studies imply that the psychosis, an ill-fated event falling across the path of human growth and development, is essentially unrelated to the essence of maturation, and that prognosis is determined by the state of social development achieved prior to the psychotic episode.

The fact that some individuals who have been psychotic may continue to grow as human beings is not a new observation, and it is startling to recall that some workers emphasized this fact prior to the advent of the major somatic therapies. Sullivan, for instance, focusing on the significance of the patient's experience of psychosis, accounts for outcome in the following manner.

> If the conservative reorganization of complexes and sentiments, which appears to underlie a goodly share of the early schizophrenic phenomenology, leads the patients to a foreconscious belief that he can circumvent or rise above environmental handicaps, and if this belief is the presenting feature of a comprehensive mental integration, his recovery proceeds. If no such reconstruction is accomplished, the patient does not recover.[4]

Similarly, Mayer-Gross attempted to account for the "course of the acute psychoses" by categorizing the possible outcomes.[5] He too felt that the way in which the psychotic episode was assimilated by the individual played a significant role in the determination of prognosis. The least favorable outcome he characterized by total denial of the entire event, the most favorable by a kind of "integration" of the experience into the ongoing life of the individual in such a way that the "challenge of continuity" was preserved. For Mayer-Gross, "continuity" could be achieved with or without growth or "melting" of the experience with the core or existence values of the patient. Continuity without growth would include such outcomes as total denial of the psychosis, hopeless despair, or substitution of chronic physical complaints in the aftermath of the psychotic experience. With growth one might achieve a genuine continuity, without exclusion of the experience. Whether or not we can accurately paraphrase Mayer-Gross in the language of ego psychology, the comparison seems clear enough. We might say that the acute psychosis, among other altered states, sets up a "search for synthesis," and that synthesis may be achieved in ways that may or may not promote ego development.[6] Recently, retrospective evidence has been obtained which shows that those individuals who are able to integrate their psychotic experience (in the sense that Mayer-Gross used the term) do in fact have better post-hospital adjustments.[7] The suggestion here is not only that social competence at the time of the illness can affect outcome but that, in addition, the psychotic episode itself can be seen as a growth struggle whose ultimate intrapsychic representation has much to do with subsequent adjustment. We will trace some of the evidence in support of this argument and point to some criteria from which to view growth possibilities latent in the acute psychosis.

ACCOUNTS FROM PATIENTS

Many patients regard their psychotic experience in retrospect as one which involved a struggle for growth and maturation. We found that a significant number of our

patients, when interviewed in a follow-up study, characterized their psychotic experience in this fashion.[7] Individuals who have written about their psychotic experience have made similar claims. Commenting upon his
psychotic episode Krim states:

> I needed an excuse to force some sort of balance
> between my bulging inner life and my timid
> outer behavior . . . We can be grateful that the
> human soul is so constructed that it ultimately
> burst concepts once held as true out of this ter-
> rible need to live and creates the world anew
> just in order to breathe in it.[8]

A very sensitive anonymous author lists some of the
personality changes that occurred during the course of
several psychotic episodes as including loss of a chronic
premorbid anxiety, a shift from a masochistic to a non-
masochistic emotional orientation, loss of excessive dependency on others, a greater capacity for warmth and
interest in people, a deeper sense of human equality, im-
provement in sexual function, freer use of intellectual
capacities and a capacity for religious experience.[8]
Norma McDonald (pseudonym), a recovered schizophrenic, wrote:

> Living with schizophrenia can be living in
> hell . . . but seen from another angle it can be
> really living, for it seems to thrive on art and
> education, it seems to lead to a deeper under-
> standing of people and living for people . . .[8]

Anton Boisen, perhaps more than anyone, paid attention to the possibility of growth potential inherent
in various forms of psychosis. His ideas are all the more
relevant because of his personal involvement in the
question. He states:

This survey of the wilderness of the lost tends
to support the hypothesis with which we
started, that many of the more serious psychoses are essentially problem-solving experiences which are closely related to certain types
of religious experience . . . we have also discovered that such ideas are not to be found in
all cases but only in those who are trying to
face their difficulties . . . We may therefore draw
the conclusion that such disturbances are not
necessarily evils but, like fever or inflammation
in the physical organism, they are attempts by
regression to lower levels of mental life to as-
similate certain hitherto unassimilated masses
of life experience. They represent the deli-
quescence of the old sets and attitudes which
make possible new formations. They are essentially purposive; in this group we even found
individuals whose lives had been changed for
the better.[9]

We have noted in the accounts presented that individuals often covertly communicated their growth strivings
in material written just prior to an acute psychotic episode. Not only are patients sometimes seemingly aware
at various levels of the growth issues involved in acute
psychosis, they also experience many of the cognitive
and affective shifts which may accompany certain forms
of major personality re-orientation. Thus creative experience, religious conversion, and other "peak experiences" may involve much of the affective lability and
"psychedelic" form of inner experience which can accompany the acute psychotic reaction. Psychotic experiences, by creating upheaval at the very core of the individual, may offer, in some instances, opportunities for

psychological growth potentially greater than those in some neurotic states and character disorders where certain defensive patterns may be relatively fixed. It appears that,

> Psychedelic and psychotomimetic phenomena are closely related. Our hypothesis is that these states demonstrate to varying degrees the subjective phenomena of intrapsychic alteration, that they are fluid states whose outcome is determined by both intrapsychic and environmental factors. There are clearly quantitative, interindividual differences in the ways such experiences can be tolerated, interpreted, terminated, and assimilated into the ongoing context of experiences.[6]

Further, if the "psychedelic" insight frequently seen at the onset of certain psychoses is illusory, such illusion cannot be disqualified from forming in whole or in part the basis of a workable illusion or vision for the future. That is, such experience can be seen as prophetic, hopeful, a glimpse of potentiality. There may be

> a relationship between pathological disillusion and illusion and disillusion as normal processes playing an essential part in the establishment of external object relations and the development of a creative relation to the world.[10]

Finally, whereas patients may see psychosis as involving the potential achievement of growth and including some of the cognitive and affective experiences of major personality alteration, they also seem to regard the psychosis itself as essentially a growth impasse, or deadlocked struggle. Time and again this idea is expressed in patient accounts. Ronald Laing has discussed the nature of the intrapsychic struggle in certain schizoid patients in his book *The Divided Self*. Kaplan reports that one individual expressed the idea of growth impasse, stating, "I cannot escape it—I cannot face it—how can I endure it?" Another, somewhat poetically, seemed to be expressing a similar kind of inner dilemma:

> When Madness comes—a strange anesthesia follows. A sleep akin to death, but more mysterious. A rest from the dim regions of unconsciousness—a state which is neither death nor living; lethal, mysterious—evil perhaps to some, but only to those who do not know the blind, intolerable horror that comes from seeing something which cannot be borne—nor escaped.[8]

The emphasis here should be on the fact that attempting to face and endure is as much a part of the inner struggle as the desire to escape. Frequently neither growth nor regression is the entire matter, and it may make a difference whether therapists focus on growth strivings or avoidance tendencies. Better still, how can we learn properly to assess and foster the former while taking appropriate account of the latter?

Similarly, if acute psychosis can be seen as a growth struggle, chronic psychosis may be viewed as an unsuccessful struggle toward continuing development. This view has been supported by information obtained in amytal interviews with chronically hospitalized patients. These individuals, often mute, under amytal seemed preoccupied with events at the time of their initial psychotic episode, which was often many years before.[11]

Therefore, I am suggesting that the essence of the acute psychosis is impasse and stalemate in human growth, and implicit in this notion is a collision of both progressive and retrogressive forces. In fact, the literature on prognostic factors shows that the intensity surrounding the acute episode is a favorable prognostic sign, suggesting that the impetus for growth is greater in such instances. All clinicians know the ominous portent of a psychosis where the onset is insidious. It is as if the relative force of the collision during growth presages the strength of the determination to push on later.

ACCOUNTS FROM THERAPISTS

Thus far we have argued that, from the subjective, experiential point of view, many psychoses have the form and content of growth struggles which have reached an impasse. However, not only patients but also some therapists have noted progressive aspects of certain acute psychotic episodes. Jackson and Watzlawick have reported a case in which the psychosis was seen and interpreted as a crisis in growth by the therapists involved.[12] Carlson has described an "acute confusional state," sometimes seen in adolescents, as a stage in ego development which is potentially maturational.[13] Particularly noteworthy are two cases reported by French and Kasanin. These cases were followed with minimal treatment for a number of years and their outcome was characterized not only by loss of psychotic symptoms, but by clear personality growth. Of interest is the observation that neither case would have been predicted to do well based on premorbid variables alone. In both cases the authors refer to a "constructive impulse to solve the problem of reconciling conflicting needs." Indeed, with these two cases in mind, the authors come to the rather remarkable conclusion that:

> In attempting to estimate the probable outcome of a psychosis, it is helpful to try to reconstruct the problem in adaptation which the psychosis is attempting to solve and then to estimate the possibilities for a successful solution in view of the actual life situation of the patient. Such an estimate is probably more important than the form of the psychosis as an index of prognosis.[14]

Minimum Requirements for Growth

In one sense, the vicissitudes of human growth are highlighted as a result of the phenomenon of psychosis. As is so often the case, a malfunctioning system lays bare the intricacy of inner structure and gives rise to renewed respect for and understanding of the function of component parts. Psychotic reactions, seen as manifestations of impasse in a struggle for growth, point to some of the truly rate-limiting processes in growth. Some capacities seem to be crucial simply for growth potential to exist at all.

One of these seems to be the presence during development of some constructive relationship between felt need and object gratification. This basic groundwork for future transactions between the human organism and his object environment must be seen as essential for growth. Prior to all other qualifying statements about object relations lies the prerequisite that the growing human organism seek and achieve relationships with the external world. Rycroft puts this principle as follows:

> It is Winnicott's contention, I believe, that early infancy is such a critical phase and that

the importance of the early mother-infant relationship lies not only in the amount of satisfaction received by the infant but also in the degree of correspondence between the infant's latent impulses, wishes, or needs and the mother's provision of the kind of stimuli necessary for their release. Insofar as the mother arouses the infant's expectations and maintains them by a modicum of satisfaction, its perception and conception of reality will accord with the pattern of its inherent instinctive tendencies, and impulses will not merely tend to be directed toward an external reality which is subjectively felt to be good but will actually be developmentally bound to the images of the reality that has released them.[10]

By contrast, in chronic psychotic states, it could be said of a patient

That he cathected the process of thinking itself and derived pleasure from passively watching his intellectual processes idling in neutral . . . the thoughts which in psychical truth have become bereft of significance come to be regarded as precisely the only objects to have any significance.[10]

The classic papers of Jonathan Lang (pseudonym, himself a paranoid schizophrenic) substantiate the impression that in psychosis affectivity becomes centered around ideation instead of external objects, thus short-circuiting the relationship between felt need and object gratification which is crucial for psychological growth. White may be dealing with an aspect of this principle when he discusses the importance of a "feeling of efficacy" in development. He notes that "we learn about reality by exploring it and by experiencing the consequences'' and adds,

> I believe that this feeling of efficacy is one of our most fundamental and biologically important affects, the basis of our persisting attempts to achieve whatever mastery we can over the environment, the thing that lies behind our unceasing attempts to enlarge the sphere of our competence. It is the root of the sense of competence that is so central in self esteem.[15]

White feels that the lack of a sense of efficacy is a central factor in the schizophrenic life style.

> Poor direction of attention and action, poor mastery of cognitive experience, weak assertiveness in interpersonal relations, low feelings of efficacy and competence, a restricted sense of agency in leading one's life—all these crop out in almost every aspect of the schizophrenic disorder.[15]

Thus I would suggest that the impasse in growth which a psychotic episode represents may ultimately promote continuing personality development if the individual does not abandon the struggle of engaging objects for the satisfaction of inner needs. When the psychosis leaves a serious paranoid experiential style—such that the object world is seen as pervasively nongratifying and menacing—or when massive withdrawal from striving takes over (certain ''hebephrenic'' reactions), we might expect prognosis to be relatively poor. The reader will recall that we have noted in the individual accounts that conflict and growth strivings are differentially represented. We have suggested that the felt experience of conflict is an important prognostic feature in these conditions.

To evaluate psychotic experiences with regard to evidence of growth potential is not necessarily to be overly optimistic about the phenomenon of psychosis. It may allow us to be more precisely optimistic where the clinical data warrant, however, and urge us to re-examine our therapeutic strategies so that we foster growth whenever possible.

GROWTH-SUPPORTING TREATMENT

We have suggested that some psychoses, when examined from the standpoint of the existential situation and experience of the patient, can be seen as impasses in human growth. What are the implications of this view for a treatment aimed at supporting the continuation of growth? To begin with, it seems appropriate that therapists devote at least as much time trying to understand what the patient is trying to accomplish as they routinely do to describing his handicaps. There is clearly inherent in most of us a certain resistance to looking at the adaptive capabilities of patients. This is an interesting phenomenon in itself, but for the present discussion it is sufficient to point to it and to urge that clinical assessment of psychotic patients include an evaluation of growth potential. In some instances the patient's strivings will be relatively clear; in others they will be fragmented and unapparent. Both Sullivan and Boisen call attention to the fact that "catatonic" patients and others with intense religious ideation are often most clearly struggling (frequently at a conscious level) with growth issues. We have noted how such conflicts may be manifest in material patients have written. At other times, skilled clinical assessment of the status of the patient's relationships with important loved ones (parents, sexual objects, siblings) may lay bare the essential conflict. Further, the patient should be made aware of the fact that his therapists view him not simply as having had an illness or "breakdown," but as being essentially involved in important purposive activity that has gone awry.

Finally, there are patients, primarily those called "hebephrenic," "process schizophrenics," or "poor premorbids," who may appear least understandable in terms of the growth model presented here. Far from being caught in a bind of progressive and retrogressive strivings, these individuals appear peculiarly illequipped and poorly motivated to master the minimal social concomitants of biological maturation. Under such circumstances, in promoting growth one may have to fall back upon elemental processes referred to above. A therapeutic program which offers long-term support and fosters—even demands—interaction with real people and activities can prevent severe regression and foster new social learning, slow but genuine enough.

In conclusion, prognosis in acute psychotic reactions is likely a result of multiple influences. Premorbid social factors and certain characteristics of the acute episode have been shown to be important. Most studies have implied that prognosis may be relatively predetermined and not particularly affected by contingencies (including treatment) related to individual assimilation of the psychotic experience. Nevertheless, as we have attempted to show from patient accounts, a case can be made for viewing some psychotic episodes as essentially maturational struggles and for viewing prognosis as, in part, related to relative success or failure in dealing with such struggles. Proper therapeutic assistance should take into account the maturational strivings inherent in many psychotic episodes.

10. Implications for Theory and Treatment of Psychotic States

IMPLICATIONS FOR THEORY

The main purpose of this book has been to present patient accounts in an effort to illustrate the experiential structure of psychotic consciousness. Thus, as a series of records, the material stands by itself and in certain respects resists analysis or interpretation. On the other hand, we have attempted to show that the accounts suggest a certain structure which has implications for the theory and treatment of psychotic states. We will first examine the theoretical implications.

A psychosis is an emergent phenomenon. It represents an *event* within a *process,* an event whose timing and characteristics are determined by four generic factors. In discussing these factors our purpose is general rather than specific. We hope to sketch in broad outline those ingredients which make up a comprehensive view of psychosis relevant to theory and clinical care. No attempt is made to deal thoroughly with the literature from any one contributing area. Our main endeavor is to point out the meshing, the interdigitation of the pieces of a behavioral puzzle. We deal somewhat more extensively with the concept of the psychotic altered state of consciousness since, in our view, this is a relatively unheralded aspect of psychosis which is largely overlooked by several comprehensive theories. For example, acute psychotic decompensation is often not regarded as an aspect of schizophrenia which merits separate theoretical attention. Most of the literature, particularly the psychological literature, focuses upon presumed enduring cognitive or behavioral traits in psychosis and, in our view, tends to overlook emergent events in the *process*, namely acute psychosis, which is the more visible clinical phenomenon.

The first factor we shall mention is difficult to define precisely, and relates to meanings usually subsumed under the concept of individual personality or character structure. Inherent in the concept of personality is the idea that within individuals there exist relatively fixed, differentiated, enduring behavior patterns which may be identified. It is assumed that these patterns of behavior are generated as the result of an interaction over developmental time between certain biological "givens" and external social influences. The notion of personality implies differential stages of fluidity in such behavioral patterning tending in the direction of relative fixity as development proceeds. Although we may not be able to define a "prepsychotic personality," we would want to acknowledge that certain noteworthy behavioral traits appear to characterize the premorbid and intermorbid lifestyle of some individuals who suffer psychotic disorders. Klein and Gittelman-Klein have focused upon the determining effect of childhood asociality.[1] Burnham has termed such individuals "undifferentiated."[2] Freeman focuses upon the relative difficulty such individuals have in the formation of intimate human relationships.[3] Rosenthal has summarized much of the work in this area and emphasizes a host of character traits such as low energy level, shyness, seclusiveness, and asociality—traits which may be included in the generic term *introversion*.[4] A relatively great degree of difficulty in moving successfully through the prolonged period of human dependency and in the formation of relatively self-regulating individuality in a social context is implied in these and other similar formulations. Speculation regarding the etiology of these personality traits has not been particularly extensive. Otto Will understands the psychotic individual's fear of human relatedness essentially as a learned aversive response, originating from early interaction with an overwhelming, persistently intrusive mother.[5] Lidz, Fleck, Wynne and other students of family interaction in psychotic disorders see the psychotic individual as the prior recipient of a variety of forms of persistent, irrational, and maladaptive instruction about the nature of interpersonal reality.[6/7] The existence of certain early critical periods for the initiation and later consolidation of adaptive social outreach and responsiveness is certainly indicated by the observations of Spitz and Provence in infants,[8/9] and by the experimental work of Harlow and his associates with infant monkeys.[10] The entire concept of "attachment behavior" has recently been reviewed by Bowlby from an ethological viewpoint.[11] The rich and protracted process of development of human social behavior from infancy to adulthood would seem most relevant to understanding the clinical observations about disturbed social behavior in psychotic disorders.

Less consideration has been given to the neurobiological prerequisites for adaptive social learning, but such factors are undoubtedly worthy of consideration and, if present, must be effective in concert with social-environmental factors. As we have suggested before, object relations must first be sought out if they are to be consolidated. Such basic processes as relatively fearless exploration of the environment must have important, if multiple, neurobiological determinants. Meehl has postulated an "integrative neural defect" or "schizotaxia" as a genetic or biological given which, under certain unfavorable nurturing or developmental experiences, leads to the "schizotype."[12] The "schizotype," according to Meehl, thus *learns* social anhedonia, interpersonal aversiveness, "cognitive slippage," and ambivalence as a result of defective equipment plus unfavorable training. Meehl sees the "schizophrenogenic mother" as pushing the schizotypic individual into decompensation, but does not consider possible novel neurobiologic processes implicated in the phenomenology of acute psychosis as distinct from the prepsychotic personality. The "drive theories" of schizophrenia have recently been reviewed by Epstein and Coleman.[13] As these authors note, such theories "share in common the assumption that a basic defect in schizophrenia consists of a low threshold for disorganization under increasing stimulus input." This defect, suggesting a basic neurobiologic etiology, is seen as playing a persistent role in development and as primarily determining the ultimate personality traits of individuals diagnosed as schizophrenic. No differentiation is made between a neural defect acting over time and contributing to personality formation as contrasted with one which might explain susceptibility to acute psychotic disorganization. At the other extreme, hyperactivity in children may lead to impaired social development when impulse dyscontrol and aggressive behavior are excessive. Rado's formulation that psychotic individuals have an impaired capacity for experiencing pleasurable gratification suggests certain neurobiological hypotheses related to reward substrates which could be relevant to motivation at a basic level.[14] This idea, also discussed by Meehl, has been set forth and pursued recently by Stein and Wise.[15] These investigators have identified a neurochemical system subserving a reward response capacity and have speculated as to biochemical means whereby this system might become inoperative. The prepsychotic personality—its liabilities, deficits, and tendencies—thus comprises one piece of the structure of human psychosis. Whatever the specific personality characteristics which may come to have general relevance in these disorders, the essential point to be made here is simply that enduring behavioral traits are one differentiated aspect of the problem of psychosis and that these traits are generally understood as deriving from a nature-nurture interaction over developmental time.

The second factor relates to the developmental process itself. As we have seen from the preceding accounts, certain invariable demands of the adolescent experience seem to contribute to the timing of the onset of psychotic disorders. The young personality which has, by gifts and experience, been adequately readied for these developmental challenges, manages some degree of mastery during this period and achieves thereby some adaptive, workable degree of human adulthood. Capacities to bear loneliness and loss, to reach for human relatedness and endure its vicissitudes, to persevere in autonomous activity and be effective in it, to restructure relationships with parental figures, and to offer affection and support to peers, as well as to solicit such caring behavior from them—all are put to test during this crucial transitional period. In many ways, it is at this stage of development that the essence of full humanity crystallizes.

The third factor which the accounts reveal has to do with the immediate interpersonal events attending the onset of psychotic behavior. Initial separation from parental figures, beginning sexual exploration, rejection in a love relationship, becoming a parent, and impasse in a marital relationship are some of the "stresses" which surround the onset of psychotic disorders. These "precipitants" are not specific to psychotic disorders alone, however. These circumstances can be seen as the triggering events which—occuring at a certain period in the development of an individual with specific personality liabilities—usher in the psychotic episode. Thus the issues of prepsychotic personality, developmental stage, and precipitating circumstances can be seen as determining the timing and content of the psychotic episode, as described in the patient accounts. To account for the actual complete emergence of psychotic behavior, however, we are left with a fourth and final factor—the psychotic altered state of consciousness.

The notion of the psychotic altered state of consciousness as an important conceptual piece of the problem of psychosis has been repeatedly stressed in this book, for it has been our purpose to highlight this idea through the patient accounts and to describe its articulation with the other three factors described above. I believe that this concept represents a crucial link between psychosocial and neurobiological theorizing related to psychotic states and provides the key to a modern, eclectic view of these disorders. We will not attempt to review the relevant neurobiological literature dealing with psychotic states. For those unfamiliar with it, however, we shall introduce this literature particularly as it pertains to possible mechanisms underlying psychotic altered states of consciousness.

The essence of the present thesis is that psychosis cannot be explained solely as a summary event resulting from prepsychotic personality pattern, developmental period, and specific stressful circumstances. These factors contribute to but do not in themselves explain the phenomenon of psychosis. *Psychotic consciousness represents the experiential pole of an altered pattern of central nervous system functioning.* Within moderate limits it manifests a reasonably reproducible phenomenology characterized by marked changes in interoceptive and exteroceptive sensory experience such that perception of self and external world undergo profound destructuring in a sensorium which is otherwise relatively clear.

It is significant that a psychotic altered state of consciousness can be produced by a relatively limited number of pharmacological compounds, and these compounds seem to be those which are in some way related to the function of the indoleamines (such as serotonin)[16] and catecholamines (such as dopamine and norepinephrine)[17] in the central nervous system. Earlier controversy concerning whether or not a particular drug did or did not produce a "model psychosis" tended to overlook the multifaceted nature of clinical psychotic states.[18] Many researchers who argued that acute drug reactions did not mimic clinical schizophrenia, for example, were focusing upon more enduring aspects of the psychotic personality ("psychotic character"). However, when "psychotic consciousness" is highlighted in the human process of clinical psychosis, then the question of psychotomimesis by drugs become more clearly focused and more plausible. [19] The relationship between mechanisms responsible for such defects as postulated by Meehl's integrative neural defect or by the drive theories of the psychological tradition and liability to psychotic consciousness is unclear. It is conceivable that some basic neural system defect is operative throughout the life of an individual prone to psychosis and is simply greatly exaggerated during acute psychosis. It is equally plausible that both processes ("psychotic character" and "psychotic consciousness'') or either process alone has its own separate, underlying neural process. In the discussion of current conceptual models below, we focus upon the phenomenon of "psychotic consciousness." However, such processes might also be pertinent to the genesis of "psychotic character."

The central nervous system appears to possess a latent capacity, neurobiologically speaking, for a pattern of functioning which experientially is human "psychotic consciousness." This concept of altered brain function in psychosis is an important departure from classical notions of "organicity," induced either by drugs or other processes. It is a concept of patterned dysfunction according to inherent structure, not primarily a deficit state. Understanding the nature of individual liability to such states would enable us to specify the nature of an "end organ deficit" in psychotic disorders and would be a major contribution to the neurobiology of altered states of consciousness. Since this is an issue of some importance, I would like to describe some of the neurobiological models currently being studied as possible mechanisms underlying psychotic altered states of consciousness.

In general, the neurobiological models of altered states are put forth with the assumption that the nervous system is an organ system whose variable structure and function imply control or inhibition of certain latent patterning processes and excitation of others. Much as an organist or conductor might select conditions of volume, pattern, and harmony, so the nervous system achieves myriad temporary functional structures to effect its various outputs. As research in neural structure and chemistry proceed, it may become increasingly possible to localize structurally and to specify chemically certain neuronal patterning systems within the central nervous system. By an almost infinite number of graded responses of excitation or inhibition within these neuronal patterning systems, many of which are clearly responsive to the symbolic structure of individual human experience, the human nervous system receives, evaluates, and stores sensory experience, assesses and expedites its needs and desires. If some of these systems are given to capricious, unpredictable, temporary or sustained fluctuations in excitation or inhibition, then the neuronal pattern undergoes alteration and the sensory and cognitive concomitants of that pattern become manifest and overriding. A neurophysiologic model which may be illustrative in this regard is that of Flynn, Chi, Bandler and associates with regard to the mechanisms underlying attack behavior in the cat.[20] These investigators have shown that the "patterning" which is imposed upon the nervous system during electrical stimulation of various attack points includes clear biasing of sensory and reflex mechanisms in favor of perceiving and biting a rat. The central stimulation thus imposes an "altered state," if you will, which preempts sensory and motor processes for a specific behavioral output throughout the duration of the stimulation. Similar sensory and cognitive biasing may occur as a result of hypothetical neural processes in psychosis which impose the patterning whose phenomenology we have described under the concept of the psychotic altered state of consciousness.

There are a variety of current models to account for the neurobiological changes leading to the altered consciousness which periodically characterizes psychotic states. One of these might be termed the concept of the circulating psychotomimetic substance. This concept suggests that the psychotic state may be an autointoxication whereby the body either erroneously manufactures or fails to inactivate certain chemical substances which then, in a fashion unregulated by physiological neural processes, react with sensitive neuronal receptor sites. Many of the molecules hypothetically implicated in such processes are amines bearing critical methyl groups, as are the compounds which produce psychotomimetic effects when administered exogenously.[21] Research has focused upon mechanisms whereby amine substances may be abnormally synthesized or inadequately degraded. An enzyme capable of adding methyl groups to physiological amines has been found in human plasma, red cells, and blood platelets,[22] and some research groups have found psychotomimetic amine substances in the urine of psychotic patients.[23] Relative deficiency of monoamine oxidase, an enzyme important in the degradation of amines, has recently been found in the platelets of certain psychotic patients.[24] Abnormal concentrations of physiologic or psychotomimetic amines might exert their effects by stimulating or inhibiting normal or hypersensitive neural receptor sites. Studies by Bunney, Goodwin, Post and co-workers on the "switch mechanism" involved in behavioral change from normality or depression to mania, provide convincing evidence that such individuals are biochemically predisposed to altered behavioral states. Increased amounts of physiologically active catecholamines or increased sensitivity of catecholamine receptor sites appear implicated in these individuals.[25] If mechanisms such as these are ultimately found to be operative in the production of psychotic consciousness in man, it will still be necessary to elucidate their relationship to the vicissitudes of stress, defense and conflict resolution within a developmental framework.

A second model to account for liability to psychotic consciousness is the receptor hypersensitivity model. This hypothesis proposes that the altered neural subtrate, rather than being a psychotomimetic neurochemical, is a receptor which is abnormally reactive. The concept of receptor hypersensitivity is an intriguing one since it has long been known that one of the consequences of nonspecific damage to neuronal tissue may be increased excitability of adjacent tissue. Recently it has been shown that chemical denervation of specific pathways in the central nervous system may lead to hypersensitivity of the receptors normally innervated by these pathways. Whatever the mechanism which might initiate central receptor hypersensitivity, such a mechanism is suggested by certain idiosyncratic responses to drugs. For instance, a minority of individuals—for reasons unknown—show psychotic responses to monoamine oxidase inhibitors, tricyclic antidepressants, L-Dopa, or low doses of amphetamines. High doses of amphetamines reliably produce a paranoid psychotic syndrome under natural or experimental conditions.[26] These compounds may act directly or release neurochemicals to act upon receptors which are abnormally sensitive. A receptor hypersensitivity hypothesis implicating dopamine has recently been advanced by Klawans as relevant to schizophrenia.[27]

A third model to explain individual vulnerability to psychotic consciousness is the possibility of deficiency of or damage to a system which normally functions as an inhibitory pathway in the central nervous system. For instance, the indole-containing midbrain raphe system seems to subserve some important inhibitory or gating function for sensory stimuli. Destruction of this area of brain in rats leads to hypersensitivity to noise and touch. LSD apparently exerts its effect directly upon these neurons and markedly inhibits their firing.[28] This effect may be intimately related to the psychotomimetic capacities of this and similar compounds.

The models cited above deal primarily with possible neurochemical processes related to neuronal patterning which may determine psychotic consciousness. Equally timely are those studies which relate to the possible neuronal sites and neurophysiologic mechanisms principally involved in this patterning. One area which has been of increasing interest in this regard is limbic forebrain. For example, Nauta has described the central connections between the "limbic system-midbrain circuit," hypothalamus, and neocortex and the importance of this interconnected network to certain behavioral capacities.[29]

> Limbic forebrain appears to receive its afferents primarily through the brain stem reticular formation, more especially from the limbic midbrain area, an organization accessible to virtually all of the "cruder" sensory modalities. It [limbic forebrain] could thus, in regard to sensory functions, be interpreted as a multisensory analyzor system linked in series with the reticular analyzor systems.

Nauta further states that the limbic forebrain system also subserves important integrating mechanisms which encompass

> neural organizations governing complex behavioral patterns, especially those subserving the preservation of the individual and the species. Such forms of behavior often show a definite line of progression which leads from alertness, "attention-focusing," and visceral-endocrine adjustments, to the full-fledged massive behavioral discharge characteristic of fighting, flight, food procurement, or sexual behavior.

Yet a third property of the limbic forebrain system described by Nauta is that of a motivational mechanism, underlying

> temporal stability in behavior, in other words, continuity of behavior or even behavioral perseverance . . . This mechanism becomes manifest at the sensorial level by "vital feelings" (comfort versus discomfort; hunger versus satiation) and often finds its outward expression in so-called affective or emotional behavior with characteristic visceral and endocrine accompaniments.

A system capable of complex sensory analysis, regulation of crucial behavioral patterns, and able to set motivational "tone" would appear possibly linked either to aspects of "psychotic consciousness" or "psychotic character" as described herein. We have previously noted the broad range of sensory alterations which obtain in psychotic states. These changes are characterized by novel but personally relevant *content* which emanates from a new pattern or *form* of sensory experience. With regard to "psychotic character," some basic issue of defective behavioral perseverance or motivation—particularly with regard to activity level or interpersonal interaction—may be related to dysfunction of limbic forebrain.

The best known clinical model for a neurophysiologically induced altered state of consciousness is that of temporal lobe (or limbic) epilepsy. Such disorders are characterized by striking alterations in the form and content of consciousness. Indeed, experimental studies involving temporal lobe stimulation of subjects have produced dramatic shifts in consciousness and have demonstrated a relationship between form and content in such experimentally induced states similar to that which we have noted in our patient accounts. That is to say, the altered *form* of consciousness thus evoked often permits the emergence of dynamic material related to conflict and defense which is specific for the individual.[30] In this regard, the association of temporal lobe seizure disorders and psychiatric symptoms, particularly psychosis, has received a great deal of attention. Of special interest is the fact that patients with temporal lobe epilepsy have shown interictal psychotic behavior in a number of instances.[31] Further, tumors of the limbic system have also been associated with a clinical diagnosis of schizophrenia.[32]

Stevens has recently reviewed the relationship between psychosis and temporal lobe disorders and concludes that, in the majority of instances, clinical psychosis is not associated with the electroencephalographic features of temporal lobe epilepsy, at least as obtained from scalp electrodes.[33] Considering other possible limbic mechanisms in psychotic states, she focuses on the relationship of the dopamine-containing nigro-striatal pathways to clinical schizophrenia, an idea originally proposed by Mettler.[34] Important recent reviews of basic and clinical data supporting a role for the nigro-striatal pathways in schizophrenia are those of Klawans[27] and Snyder.[17] In her paper, Stevens notes that the nigro-striatal pathways ascend to two forebrain regions which appear to have separate but interrelated functions related to motor and sensory integration. One of these areas, the limbic dopamine-containing system, is discussed extensively as a possible region whose function may be abnormal in some psychotic states. Stevens states,

> Compromise of the focusing and filtering functions which have been suggested for the

paleostriatum may be viewed as a release phenomenon in a horizontal plane of consciousness, leading to widening of the *field* [Stevens's italics] of awareness, a concept complementary and supplementary to the notion of vertical hierarchy and suppression of lower by higher levels, so useful in clinical neurological analysis. Pathological widening of the field of consciousness due to diminished efficiency of habituation or desensitization could engender internal incoherence which relates to the clinical pathology of schizophrenic psychoses.

Of central importance to this hypothesis is the fact that the drugs which are effective in the treatment of schizophrenia are known to have significant effects upon dopamine metabolism in the nigro-striatal pathways.[35]

Thus, whatever the ultimate mechanisms which may be shown to underlie protracted altered states of consciousness in psychosis, it is likely that such processes represent a conceptual bridge which may ultimately serve to integrate psychological and biological approaches to the understanding of psychotic states. Such an integration might have the following outline: Individual liability, developmental demand, and circumstance coalesce to produce conflict and impasse leading to the production of a psychotic altered state of consciousness in certain individuals *uniquely prone* to such alterations in consciousness. Subjective experience in these states is determined by state-related factors and by individual-specific characteristics of conflict and defense. The altered state permits the emergence of new experiential patterns. The model is thus a psychosomatic-psychic model with allowance made for the likelihood that the vulnerable personality reacting to developmental stress may itself be a characterological product of endowment and development. The altered state construct relates directly to the concept of the "defensive alteration of ego functions" of psychoanalytic structural theory,[36] but would add the proviso that certain individuals have a definable neurobiological propensity to such alterations in the face of unresolvable conflict. Thus the *degree* of anxiety engendered by conflict would not be the sole determinant of the psychotic state.

IMPLICATIONS FOR TREATMENT

If timing, content, and form are separate but interacting explanatory principles with regard to the problem of psychosis, then treatment can be addressed in a truly eclectic fashion. Using the model we propose, the altered state, current life events, and long-term growth needs can be individually assessed and addressed in a complementary manner. Expertise in each area may be brought to bear cooperatively in the individual instance. We will consider the implications which this theoretical model has for the various components of treatment.

The Altered State

In the present analysis of the structure of psychotic experience, we have suggested that there is a complex interaction of biological and psychological processes in these syndromes. Specifically, biological processes may be implicated in the propensity to altered states or in certain aspects of the prepsychotic personality such as innate deficiencies in exploratory behavior or motivated object seeking which may underlie processes of individuation and socialization. We have attempted to show that the altered state of consciousness in psychotic states permits the emergence of a variety of novel subjective experiences. We have pointed to some of the repetitiousness as well as some of the variety in the structure of these experiences. Whereas the content of acute psychotic states may be illustrative and meaningful in a psychodynamic sense, treatment requires that the patient be free of the idiosyncratic cognitive experiences which these states impose. The altered state is an emergent symptom complex and its presence prevents effective and reality-oriented growth and work between patient and therapeutic events and individuals. We occasionally hear that a patient is "just sealing over" when recovering from an acute psychotic episode as if such an outcome were to be avoided. Some current theorists have even suggested that there is something inviolate in the psychotic experience, that it is a sacred process running its course, not to be tampered with. We would agree that the onset of psychotic states is closely linked to the essence of human development and that aspects of the developmental struggle are often depicted in the content of the psychotic altered state of consciousness. However, we would maintain that the states themselves are incompatible with mastery of conflict and continued growth. Such an assertion does not mean that the psychotic episode is devoid of potential meaning for the individual (we have discussed this issue at greater length in the preceding chapter). However, this meaning is not easily assimilated nor made to work in the life of the patient. Many psychotic experiences are both indelible and seductive. Patients may relinquish the "realness" of such episodes with great reluctance, both because of their inherently convincing quality and because of the apparent order and relief which alloplastic delusional clarification brings to the self in disarray. Thus, reconnection of the patient to the developmental task is not always easy to achieve and is frequently a less exotic undertaking than other therapeutic approaches. On the other hand, although we may appropriately worry about the individual patient who appears to have no distance from his psychotic state, we might also be concerned about the individual who has forgotten too soon, who has lost whatever growth momentum may have been represented in the psychotic impasse.

Thus we are suggesting that removal of the altered state in psychosis makes possible the application of psychosocial therapies. It is a necessary and initial but rarely sufficient step in treatment. Current psychiatric training frequently fails to present a model for the treatment of psychotic disorders which allows for the full and interlocking utilization of therapies directed at the altered state and those aimed at facilitation of growth. As delineated here, management of the altered state exposes the need for and makes possible the employment of the psychosocial therapies. Presently the psychotic altered state of consciousness is the aspect of psychosis which generally responds to antipsychotic medication. There may be individuals who do not need medication, who through other therapeutic approaches can gain rapid control of the altered experiential state in psychosis. Indeed, the model proposed (that the psychotic altered state is initiated by conflict) is entirely consistent with psychotherapeutic treatment models[36] so long as it is recognized that conflict resolution can rarely be addressed while the psychotic altered state of consciousness is regnant. There are treatments, such as electroconvulsive therapy, which may rapidly obliterate psychotic symptoms but which also usually effectively isolate the patient from whatever life issues were relevant to the onset of the psychosis. By our analysis, such an effect might be considerably less desirable.

Finally, therapies which make use of induced altered states of consciousness must consider carefully the issue of form versus content. Whether the altered state is intended to be a momentous, value-changing experience[37] or designed primarily to elicit dynamic, emotionally relevant material in psychotherapy,[38] it is important to acknowledge that the presence of critical personal material in consciousness is not a guarantee that such material can be critically evaluated and utilized. Indeed, the production of altered states of consciousness outside of the realities of human endeavor and interaction may, in some individuals, seriously undercut the crucial psychobiological relationship between human affect and human relationships or activity. Thus one finds in long-term work with psychotic patients or individuals who have used mind-altering substances extensively, that altered states of consciousness may become egosyntonic and function essentially as entrenched defensive structures which serve to insulate the individual from cognitive and emotional realities.[39] Even when the altered state itself has been interdicted through the use of therapeutic medication, one may find that aspects or fragments of the altered state are retained in the psychological repertoire of the patient, particularly when the treatment experience during the acute episode has involved a substantial amount of secondary gain. Attempts to mobilize the patient to interpersonal or vocational activity may thus evoke a return of part or all of the patient's psychotic experience. Under these circumstances the actual status and internal representation of the experience to the patient appears different from that during the acute episode, and techniques of behavior modification and group pressure may be usefully employed at this point if antipsychotic medication has been well-regulated and stabilized.

Current Life Events

For the understanding of any psychotic patient, the present is crucial. Psychiatry has long been known to take the long view, to have an interest in early life experience. The present is frequently neglected, yet it always contains the key to the relevant past and to the foreseeable future. Our model states that psychosis may occur when the immediate configuration of forces is marshalled to exploit an individual liability in the process of continuing maturation. These forces can be quite varied but the care of the psychotic patient requires that they be understood. Sometimes these forces represent simply the emergent demands of a particular developmental stage. One learns to think of human development as a natural force that exerts real pressure. In fact, it seems difficult to explain the phenomenon of psychosis, even in the most poorly equipped individual, unless one postulates a progressive force operating in the setting of a variety of constraints. Some of these constraints are characterological, others are imposed from outside the individual. Where they are imposed by unusual circumstances constraints may be relatively obvious. A major contribution to clinical psychiatry in the past fifteen years has been the recognition that constraints to growth can be subtle and imposed by the immediate social environment, e.g., the family. In fact, one might state that treatment of current life events essentially consists of careful evaluation of the immediate social context with a view to uncovering the implicit growth constraints which may exist. It should be unnecessary to state that this assertion is not based upon the notion that the family is to blame, or some similar oversimplification. However, the family literature now richly delineates the amazing variety of constraints to growth which may evolve from strategies to maintain parental or family equilibrium or perpetuate a particular *modus operandi* which a family has developed. Proper treatment of current life events includes the uncovering of the particular close social alignment which makes continuing development problematic for an individual. It usually requires the substitution or the realignment of supportive objects in a way that consistent new support is available during prolonged periods of developmental struggle. Strategies, tactics, and treatment techniques will differ from case to case, but each approach must be based upon accurate assessment of the current social milieu of the patient. In our analysis, this work cannot begin to occur unless the patient is first free of the idiosyncratic experiences which characterize the psychotic altered state of consciousness.

Long-Term Growth

Most psychotic patients require at least the availability of supportive people or institutions for prolonged periods of time, although not necessarily continuously. Since the most crucial developmental tasks of this group lie in individuation, self-definition, and the development of a sense of social competence, the time required for progress toward these ends must be measured in years. Current therapeutic programs rarely appear to acknowledge this fact. We are not suggesting that individual intensive dyadic relationships are routinely required or even desirable for the facilitation of growth over such a protracted period. More pointedly we direct attention to the scarcity of unified programs with an acknowledged task of facilitating growth over time during late adolescence and young adulthood, the most usual period for psychotic reactions to occur. Continuity of care is of the essence for these individuals and such care need not imply large budgets and impressive physical facilities. Most public hospitals could save money by such programs of continuity since readmission rates for young psychotic patients would probably decrease. Ready access to brief hospitalization, self care units, day or night care, resocialization experiences, and vocational training are required and should ideally be included under a single administrative umbrella. We currently impede meaningful continuous support for patients by requiring that they cross administrative boundaries to receive a variety of services. Special training schools currently exist in our society which are designed to assist those with various obvious kinds of cognitive impairment such as mental retardation, blindness, and deafness. Further, special programs exist for those whose behavior results in their being called delinquent. However, few facilities define their task as the facilitation of human development as such. It may be that in the psychotic states we are beginning to identify more clearly the actual processes of human growth, development, and individuation. Once the processes of human differentiation and individuation are more completely understood, the psychotic states may bear witness to one important manner in which this most human of metamorphoses may go awry. We may then be able to speak meaningfully of the major disorders of growth and development and be prepared to offer in public institutions the special supportive and educational experiences which these conditions require. Such a step would require great courage on the part of a society, for it would rest upon a humble recognition of the necessity, complexity, and universality of the experience of human development.

Bibliography

Introduction

1. Sommer, R. & Osmond, H. Autobiographies of former mental patients. *J. Ment. Sci.*, 106:648-662, 1960 (Addendum, *J. Ment. Sci.* 107:1030-1032, 1961).
2. Macalpine, I. & Hunter, R. *Daniel Paul Schreber—memoirs of my nervous illness.* London: William Dawson and Sons Ltd., 1955.
3. Perceval, J. *A narrative of the treatment experienced by a gentleman, during a state of mental derangement.* London: Effingham Wilson, 1840.
4. Custance, J. *Wisdom, madness, and folly.* New York: Farrar, Straus & Giroux, 1952.
5. Wagner, G. *Selected writings of Gerard de Nerval* (trans.). New York: Grove Press, 1957.
6. Boisen, A. *The exploration of the inner world.* New York: Harper & Row, 1952; *Out of the depths.* New York: Harper & Row, 1960.
7. Lang, J. The other side of hallucinations. *Amer. J. Psychiat.*, 94:1090-1097, 1938; The other side of affective aspects of schizophrenia. *Psychiatry*, 2:195-202, 1939; The other side of the ideological aspects of schizophrenia. *Psychiatry*, 3:389-393, 1940.

8. Kaplan, B. *The inner world of mental illness.* New York: Harper & Row, 1964.

9. Landis, C. & Mettler, F. *Varieties of psychopathological experience.* New York: Holt, Rinehart & Winston, 1964.

10. Federn, P. *Ego psychology and the psychoses.* New York: Basic Books, 1952.

11. Searles, H. The schizophrenic individual's experience of his world. *Psychiatry,* 30:119-131, 1967.

12. McGhie, A. & Chapman, J. Disorders of attention and perception in early schizophrenia. *Brit. J. Med. Psychol.,* 34:103-116, 1961; Chapman, J. The early symptoms of schizophrenia. *Brit. J. Psychiat.,* 112: 225-251, 1966.

13. Konrad, C. *Die beginnende schizophrenie.* Stuttgart: Thieme, 1958.

14. Freud, S. Constructions in analysis. In: J. Strachey (Ed.), *Complete psychological works,* Vol. 23, pg. 267. London: Hogarth Press, 1964. I am indebted to Dr. Maurice G. Marcus for calling my attention to this passage.

1. The Altered State in Acute Psychosis

1. Mellor, C. First rank symptoms of schizophrenia. *Brit. J. Psychiat.,* 117:15-23, 1970; Taylor, M. Schneiderian first-rank symptoms and clinical prognostic features in schizophrenia. *Arch. Gen. Psychiat.,* 26:64-67, 1972.

2. Custance, J. *Wisdom, madness, and folly.* New York: Farrar, Straus & Giroux, 1952.

3. Anonymous. An autobiography of a schizophrenic experience. *J. Abnorm. Soc. Psychol.,* 51:677-680, 1955.

4. See ref. 2, *Introduction.*
5. Beers, C. *A mind that found itself.* New York: Longmans, Green, 1908, pp. 30-33.
6. McDonald, N. Living with schizophrenia. *Canad. Med. Assoc. J.,* 82:218-221, 678-681, 1960.
7. Terrill, J. The nature of the LSD experience. *J. Nerv. Ment. Dis.,* 135: 425-439, 1962.
8. Giarman, N. & Freedman, D. Biochemical aspects of the actions of psychotomimetic drugs. *Pharm. Rev.,* 17:1-25, 1965.
9. James, W. *The varieties of religious experience.* New York: The New American Library of World Literature, Inc., 1958.
10. See ref. 6, *Introduction.*
11. Laing, R. Transcendental experience in relation to religion and psychosis. *Psychedelic Rev.,* 6:7-15, 1965.
12. Maslow, A. *Toward a psychology of being.* New York: D. Van Nostrand Co., Inc., 1962.
13. Arlow, J. & Brenner, C. *Psychoanalytic concepts and the structural theory.* New York: International Universities Press, Inc., 1964.
14. Carlson, H. The relationship of the acute confusional state to ego development. *Int. J. Psychoanal.,* 42:517-536, 1961.
15. Freemantle, A. (Ed.) *Protestant mystics.* New York: New American Library of World Literature, 1965.
16. Hollister, L. Drug-induced psychoses and schizophrenic reactions: A critical comparison. *Ann. N. Y. Acad. Sci.,* 96:80-92, 1962.
17. See ref. 10, *Introduction.*
18. Deikman, A. Experimental meditation. *J. Nerv. Ment. Dis.,* 136:329-343, 1963; Kris, E. *Psychoanalytic explorations in art.* New York: International Universities Press, Inc., 1952; Miller, S. Ego auton-

omy in sensory deprivation, isolation, and stress. *Int. J. Psychoanal.*, 43:1-20, 1962; Christensen, C. Religious conversion. *Arch. Gen. Psychiat.*, 9:207-216, 1963.

19. Freud, S. *An outline of psychoanalysis.* New York: W. W. Norton & Co., Inc. 1949.

20. Loewald, H. Hypnoid states—repression, abreaction, and recollection. *J. Amer. Psychoanal. Assoc.*, 3:201-210, 1955.

8. Experiential Progression in Acute Psychosis

1. Laing, R. *The divided self.* Baltimore: Penguin Books, 1965.

2. Erikson, E. *Identity and the life cycle.* New York: International Universities Press, 1959.

3. See ref. 7, *Introduction.*

4. Todd, J. The Syndrome of Capgras. *Psychiat. Quart.*, 31:250-265, 1957.

5. See ref. 11, *Introduction.*

6. Will, O. Catatonic behavior in schizophrenia. *Contemp. Psychoanal.*, 9:29-57, 1972.

7. Burnham, D. Schizophrenia and object relations. In: D. Burnham (Ed.), *Schizophrenia and the need-fear dilemma.* New York: International Universities Press, 1969.

8. Stein, W. The sense of becoming psychotic. *Psychiatry,* 30:262-275, 1967.

9. See ref. 12, *Introduction.*

10. Freeman, T. with Cameron, J. & McGhie, A. *Studies on psychosis—descriptive, psychoanalytic, and psychological aspects.* New York: International Universities Press, 1966; Freeman, T. *Psychopathology of the psychoses.* New York: International Universities Press, 1969.

11. Silverman, J. Scanning-control mechanism and cognitive filtering in paranoid and non-paranoid schizophrenia. *J. Consult. Psychol.*, 28:385-393, 1964; The problem of attention in research and theory on schizophrenia. *Psychol. Rev.*, 71:352-379, 1964.

12. Livingston, P. & Blum, R. Attention and speech in acute schizophrenia. *Arch. Gen. Psychiat.*, 18:373-381, 1968.

13. Deikman, A. De-automatization and the mystic experience. *Psychiatry*, 29:324-338, 1966; Implications of experimentally induced contemplative meditation. *J. Nerv. Ment. Dis.*, 142:101-116, 1966.

14. White, R. The experience of efficacy in schizophrenia. *Psychiatry*, 28:199-211, 1965.

9.   Psychosis and Human Development

1. Payne, R. & Sloane, R. Can schizophrenia be defined? *Dis. Nerv. System*, 29:113-117, 1968 (supplement).

2. Vaillant, G. Natural history of the remitting schizophrenias. *Amer. J. Psychiat.*, 120:367-375, 1963.

3. Kantor, R. & Herron, W. *Process and reactive schizophrenia*. Palo Alto: Science and Behavior Books, 1966.

4. Sullivan, H. *Schizophrenia as a human process.* New York: W. W. Norton & Co., 1962.

5. Mayer-Gross, W. Uber die stellungnahme zur abgelaufenen akuten psychose. *Zeitschrift für die gesamte Neurologie und Psychiatrie*, 60:160-212, 1920.

6. Bowers, M. & Freedman, D. "Psychedelic" experiences in acute psychoses. *Arch. Gen. Psych.*, 15: 240-248, 1966.

7. Soskis, D. & Bowers, M. The schizophrenic experience: a follow-up study of attitude and post-hospital adjustment. *J. Nerv. Ment. Dis.*, 149:443-449, 1969.
8. See ref. 8, *Introduction*.
9. See ref. 6, *Introduction*.
10. Rycroft, C. *Imagination and reality*. New York: International Universities Press, 1965.
11. Ehrentheil, F. Thought content of mute catatonic schizophrenic patients. *J. Nerv. Ment. Dis.*, 137:187-197, 1963.
12. Jackson, D. & Watzlawick, P. The acute psychosis as manifestation of a growth experience. *Psychiatric Research Report 16*, 1963.
13. See ref. 14, Chapter 1.
14. French, T. & Kasanin, J. A psychodynamic study of the recovery of two schizophrenic cases. *Psychoanal. Quart.*, 10:1-22, 1941.
15. See ref. 14, Chapter 8.

10. Implications for Theory and Treatment of Psychotic States

1. Gittelman-Klein, R. & Klein, D. Premorbid asocial adjustment and prognosis in schizophrenia. *J. Psychiat. Res.*, 7:35-53, 1969.
2. See ref. 7, Chapter 8.
3. See ref. 10, Chapter 8.
4. Rosenthal, D. (Ed.) Possible inherited factors: patterns of behavioral disturbance, premorbid personality, and test performance. In: *The Genain quadruplets*. New York: Basic Books, 1963.
5. Will, O. Schizophrenia-psychological treatment. In: A. Freedman & H. Kaplan (Eds.), *Comprehensive textbook of psychiatry*. Baltimore: Williams & Wilkins, 1967.

6. Lidz, T., Fleck, S. & Cornelison, A. *Schizophrenia and the family.* New York: International Universities Press, 1965.

7. Wynne, L. & Singer, M. Thought disorder and family relations of schizophrenics: I. A research strategy. *Arch. Gen. Psychiat.,* 9:191-198, 1963; II. A classification of forms of thinking. *Arch. Gen. Psychiat.,* 9:199-206, 1963.

8. Spitz, R. *The first year of life.* New York: International Universities Press, 1965.

9. Provence, S. & Lipton, R. *Infants in institutions.* New York: International Universities Press, 1963.

10. Harlow, H. & Harlow, M. The affectional systems. In: A. Schrier, H. Harlow, & F. Stollnitz (Eds.), *Behavior of nonhuman primates,* Vol. 2. New York: Academic Press, 1965.

11. Bowlby, J. *Attachment and loss,* Vol. I. New York: Basic Books, 1969.

12. Meehl, P. Schizotaxia, schizotypy, schizophrenia. *American Psychologist,* 17:827-838, 1962.

13. Epstein, S. & Coleman, M. Drive theories of schizophrenia. In: R. Canero (Ed.), *The schizophrenic syndrome,* Vol. 1. New York: Brunner-Mazel, 1971.

14. Rado, S., Buchenholz, B., Dunton, H., Karlen, S., & Sensecu, R. Schizotypal organization: a preliminary report on a clinical study of schizophrenia. In: S. Rado & G. Daniels (Eds.), *Changing concepts of psychoanalytic medicine.* New York: Grune, 1956.

15. Stein, L. & Wise, C. Possible etiology of schizophrenia: progressive damage to the noradrenergic reward system by 6-hydroxydopamine. *Science,* 171:1032-1036, 1971.

16. Bowers, M. LSD-related states as models of psychosis. In: J. Cole, A. Freedman, & A. Friedhoff (Eds.), *Psychopathology and psychopharmacology.*

Baltimore: The Johns Hopkins University Press, 1973.

17. Snyder, S. Catecholamines in the brain as mediators of amphetamine psychosis. *Arch. Gen. Psychiat.*, 27:169-179, 1972.

18. Hollister, L. *Chemical psychosis.* Springfield: Charles C. Thomas, 1968.

19. Bowers, M. & Freedman, D. "Psychedelic" experiences in acute psychoses. *Arch. Gen. Psychiat.*, 15:240-248, 1966.

20. Flynn, J. & Bandler, R. Patterned reflexes during centrally elicited attack behavior. In: W. Field (Ed.), *The neural basis of violence and aggression.* Austin: The University of Texas Press, in press.

21. Weil-Malherbe, H. & Szara, S. *The biochemistry of functional and experimental psychoses.* Springfield: Charles C. Thomas, 1971.

22. Axelrod, J. Enzymatic formation of psychotomimetic metabolites from normally occurring compounds. *Science,* 134:343, 1961; Mandell, A. & Morgan, M. Indole(ethyl)amine-n-methyltransferase in human brain. *Nature,* 230:85-87, 1971; Saavedra, J. & Axelrod, J. psychotomimetic n-methylated tryptamines: formation in brain in vivo and in vitro. *Science,* 172:1365-1366, 1972; Narasimhachari, N., Plaut, J., & Himwich, H. Indolethylamine-n-methyltransferase in serum samples of schizophrenics and normal controls. *Life Sciences 11,* Part II, 221-227, 1972; Wyatt, R., Saavedra, J., & Axelrod, J. A dimethyltryptamine-forming enzyme in human blood. *Amer. J. Psychiat.,* 130:754-760, 1973.

23. Narasimhachari, N., Heller, B., Spaide, J., Haskovec, L., Fujimori, M., Tabushi, K., & Himwich, H. Urinary studies of schizophrenics and controls. *Biol. Psychiat.,* 3:9-20, 1971; N-N-dimethylated indoleamines in blood. *Biol. Psychiat.,* 3:21-23, 1971.

24. Murphy, D. & Weis, R. Reduced monoamine oxidase activity in blood platelets from bipolar depressed patients. *Amer. J. Psychiat.*, 128:1351-1357, 1972; Murphy, D., & Wyatt, R. Reduced monoamine oxidase activity in blood platelets from schizophrenic patients. *Nature*, 238:225-226, 1972.

25. Bunney, W., Murphy, D., Goodwin, F., Borge, G., House, K., & Gordon, E. The "switch process" in manic-depressive illness. *Arch. Gen. Psychiat.*, 27: 295-319, 1972.

26. Griffith, J., Cavanaugh, J., Held, J., & Oates, J. Detroamphetamine-evaluation of psychotomimetic properties in man. *Arch. Gen. Psychiat.*, 26:97-100, 1972; Angrist, B., Shopsin, B., & Gershon, S. Comparative psychotomimetic effects of stereoisomers of amphetamine. *Nature*, 234:152-153, 1971.

27. Klawans, H., Goetz, C., & Westheimer, R. Pathophysiology of schizophrenia and the striatum. *Dis. Nerv. System*, 33:711-719, 1972.

28. Aghajanian, G., Foote, W., & Sheard, M. LSD-sensitive neuronal units in the midbrain raphe. *Science*, 161:706-708, 1968.

29. Nauta, W. Central nervous organization and the endocrine motor system. In: A. Nalbandov (Ed.), *Advances in neuroendocrinology*. 5-21, 1963.

30. Mahl, G., Rothenberg, A., Delgado, J., & Hamlin, H. Psychological responses in the human to intracerebral electrical stimulation. *Psychosomatic Medicine*, 26:337-368, 1964; Ferguson, S., Rayport, M., Gardner, R., Kass, W., Weiner, H., & Reiser, M. Similarities in mental content of psychotic states, spontaneous seizures, dreams, and responses to electrical brain stimulation in patients with temporal lobe epilepsy. *Psychosomatic Medicine*, 31:479-497, 1969.

31. Slater, E., Beard, A., & Glitheroe, E. The schizo-

phrenia-like psychoses of epilepsy. *Brit. J. Psychiat.,* 109-95-150, 1963.

32. Malamud, N. Psychiatric disorder with intracranial tumors of the limbic system. *Arch. Neurol.,* 17: 113-123, 1967.

33. Stevens, J. An anatomy of schizophrenia? *Arch. Gen. Psychiat.,* in press.

34. Mettler, F. Perceptual capacity, functions of the corpus striatum, and schizophrenia. *Psychiat. Quart.,* 29:89-111, 1955.

35. Snyder, S., Taylor, K., Coyle, J., & Meyerhoff, J. The role of brain dopamine in behavioral regulation and the actions of psychotropic drugs. *Amer. J. Psychiat.,* 127:199-207, 1970.

36. Arlow, J. & Brenner, C. The psychopathology of the psychoses: a proposed revision. *Int. J. Psychoanal.,* 50:5-14, 1969; London, N. An essay on schizophrenia. Part I: Review and critical assessment of the development of the two theories. *Int. J. Psychoanal.,* 54:169-177, 1973; Part II: Discussion and re-statement of the specific theory of schizophrenia. 54: 179-193, 1973.

37. Savage, C. & McCabe, O. Residential psychedelic (LSD) therapy for the narcotic addict. *Arch. Gen. Psychiat.,* 28:808-814, 1973

38. Chandler, O. & Hartman, M. LSD as a facilitating agent in psychotherapy. *Arch. Gen. Psychiat.,* 6: 286-299, 1960.

39. Glass, G. & Bowers, M. Chronic psychosis associated with long-term psychotomimetic drug abuse. *Arch. Gen. Psychiat.,* 23:97-103, 1970.

Index